——— THE ———
MaxxMETHOD

W O R K B O O K

How to Love Yourself and
Become Who You Are Meant to Be

Christy Maxey, MC

Dedication

This book is dedicated to my sister Tammy and the rest of my family of origin. You are my favorite group of imperfect, hard-working and loving people.

Acknowledgments

———————————

To all my clients who have trusted me to be a small part of their pain, their happiness, and their lives, thank you. I don't take that lightly. I feel honored and privileged. You have enriched my life beyond measure.

There is nothing better than to be able to reach out to friends and family who are there for you no matter what. For support. Encouragement. Honest feedback. I am forever grateful for such people in my life. My parents, two of the most generous human beings I know. Your unconditional love is always felt and has fueled my own self-worth and self-love. My sister, Julie, who I've leaned on throughout this process. My childhood best friend, Kris, and her husband, Paul, who are the epitome of love and support. My kind and generous friend Ellen who has encouraged me from the beginning. To Gordie and Jackie for your support, encouragement, and friendship.

And to all my family, friends and clients who make me laugh because mental well-being requires laughter!

Contents

How I Became My Own Coach

I am about to tell you my story and how this workbook came into existence.

I've always been fascinated by human behavior and emotion, even as a child. No surprise to me, I pursued a bachelor's degree in psychology and a master's degree in counseling.

After two decades as a therapist in private practice, I saw many trends that were frustrating. First, the mental health field seemed to be in the dark ages. Therapy is believed to be meant for people with a "mental illness," however, most people who came to my office did not need a diagnosis. *They needed skills to deal with the everyday human experience that we all go through.*

The human experience is complicated and runs deep. However, there is no need to stigmatize and pathologize it. That is damaging.

The system is broken and limited, and it's not meant for everyone. Many people avoid therapy because they don't want to be labeled as mentally ill. Unfortunately, I have seen intelligent, successful people face many harmful consequences because they didn't seek help and/or didn't get the kind of help they needed.

Therapy and psychiatry are important and much needed for people who are suffering from true mental illness and need a diagnosis to determine treatment.

However, many people don't need a diagnosis. They need a place to go to:

1. Receive skills to increase their emotional intelligence.
2. Help deal with normal human experiences, emotions, and thinking patterns that we all go through.
3. Restore the ways we hold ourselves back from authentically loving ourselves and becoming who we are meant to be.

I want to be part of a movement that is making valuable information and knowledge readily available to everyone! I believe this type of movement will help destigmatize emotional, mental and psychological health, and serve as a necessary and effective method of prevention.

Another trend I have witnessed is that most people don't love themselves. I'm talking about people who are great mothers and fathers, excellent employees, successful business owners and top-of-their-class high school students—people who are talented and have unique skills to offer the world.

To them, none of this matters. They never feel good enough. They don't value themselves. They don't believe they deserve love—and on and on. They simply don't like themselves and they don't know how to get there.

These core beliefs of "I'm not good enough," "I'm not worthy," and "I don't deserve love" are myths that have enormous negative effects on self-worth, self-esteem, relationships, level of happiness, and life fulfillment.

My mission is to increase the world's self-worth, one person at a time. I want to help people build a foundation of self-worth, love themselves, and see the importance and benefits of it. We are all born valuable, and we're needlessly wasting time suffering in self-doubt, self-loathing, and self-judgment. All of this leads to depression, anxiety, shame, anger, relationship problems, and living small lives. After two decades of working with thousands of people, I have seen very closely the devastation of not knowing how to love ourselves.

I know there is a way to help people make deeper, longer-lasting change. Where do people go to get help with everyday issues, problems, and conditions that all of us experience throughout our lives?

My own experience with therapy

About three years ago, I experienced some intense difficulties in my life. I lost a close sister to cancer, and my family experienced hardships and tragedies that greatly affected me. I turned to therapy, as I always do when I hit a rough patch.

Something happened that I didn't expect. Each session fell flat. I felt worse leaving each session than when I went in. I felt lost, anxious, depressed, stagnant, stuck, and lonely. I knew I needed something different.

I understood why so many people avoid therapy. They aren't mentally ill, and they don't want to think that something is wrong with them.

I was right there with them. Pathologizing myself and/or remaining stuck in blame for my unfortunate life experiences just wasn't the road I wanted to take. And, quite frankly, nothing happened in any of those sessions, and I left feeling that it was a waste of my time and money.

The turning point: Becoming my own coach

One day, feeling frustrated that time with my therapist was not helping, I remember sitting in my car and thinking, *What do I do with my clients?* I prided myself in helping my clients get the results they were looking for as effectively and efficiently as I could. It dawned on me that I could do the same for myself.

I finally decided to take my pain into my own hands, and I did what I'm offering you in this workbook. I vetted the strategies that I used when helping people over and over again in my private practice, and I used them on myself.

I became my own coach.

For two months straight, every day, I went to work on myself dealing with whatever emotional state showed up that day.

Each morning, I used the strategies that are in this workbook, and I began to find my way out of the darkness. (Which by the way, none of us are exempt from.)

What was surprising was that I discovered all kinds of things that I *wasn't* expecting.

I discovered a world of coaching that was full of innovative, energetic problem solvers. I discovered that traditional therapy felt like the "slow boat to China." I wasn't interested in that path anymore, not for me or my clients. This workbook offers you a lifelong coaching solution of loving yourself by building a foundation of self-worth.

Once you learn the essential tools and strategies, you can use them at any time, in any place: when life hits, when you experience anxiety, when a relationship becomes challenging, when you experience a loss, and so on. This workbook will always bring you back to yourself. This is where the magic happens. Change doesn't occur when you're focused on others; change happens when you focus on yourself.

The best part is that you can use these strategies and tools even when life is going well. Learning the tools, methods, and concepts will not only help you out of your suffering, but it will also help you bring greater joy or success into your life.

Personal development is not a destination. Personal development is truly a journey. If you choose to travel this road, you can level up in a way that continually challenges you to live your best life.

This workbook is a culmination of what I know from my education, training, and experience. I've put into it what I believe to be the most succinct, effective, and efficient methods to make changes in your life. Efficiency is important to me; therefore, I made this as simple as I could.

I want people to learn the necessary skills in being a human. I want people to learn to be responsible for their own psychological health. I want them to learn emotional resilience and how to thrive. I want people to heal as quickly as possible so they can live their lives in a way that brings them greater happiness, joy, love, and success.

I've noticed that some things that people do to feel better are surface actions, kind of like cutting the weed but not getting the root, so the problems keep growing back. True healing requires building a foundation with mindfulness, self-compassion, self-acceptance. True healing gets to the root and leads to transformation.

Your life is meant to be enjoyed! And, building a foundation of true self-worth is not that difficult.

The MaxxMETHOD - Twenty-plus years in the making

Internally and psychologically we are driven by three forces: our emotions, our thoughts, and our wants (which includes desires, dreams, goals, etc.). I learned early in my career that we cannot change anything until we first become aware of what is going on inside us.

In over twenty-one years as a therapist and coach, I have witnessed over and over how our thoughts, emotions, and dreams (or lack of dreams) fuel our self-esteem, self-worth, mood, and actions. In that time, I've never known anyone who was able to change or heal their thoughts and emotions until they become mindful of them.

People come to me when they are ready to make changes. I can hear it in their voices. They are tired of the way they feel, yet they're not sure how to change it. I can tell when they're ready to commit to the work necessary to excavate the past, learn new skills, heal, and create a new future.

I have created a simple, six-pronged method to teach the most important concepts necessary in personal development. The six elements of the MaxxMETHOD are:

- **M**indfulness
- **E**motions
- **T**houghts
- **H**ealing
- **O**wn Your Dreams
- **D**o It Now!

When we can master these elements and integrate them into our lives, we can then create and design the life we want.

When I began my own self-healing, I was committed to changing where I was. I knew I wanted to feel better, to feel different. I worked at it every day for two months.

The first few weeks were extremely difficult. They were emotionally painful. I was addressing grief and loss, and I let myself be there. I knew it was the only way through the emotions, so I made a commitment to myself.

As time went on, I began to feel different. My sorrow began to lift. My self-defeating thoughts began to shift. I began to grow, to feel hope, and to love again.

As I've built my coaching business and while writing this workbook, I can honestly say that using the METHOD has led to greater self-love in myself—and the benefits that come along with that. Those are your rewards for your commitment to yourself. I have always told my clients that the most important relationship you have is the one with yourself. This workbook is for you.

I decided to use the MaxxMETHOD framework to focus on the most universal problem that I saw in most of my clients: finding self-love and self-worth and becoming who you are meant to be.

Let's face it, life is difficult sometimes and we occasionally lose our way.

You are worthy and valuable—just for being you. You just may not know it yet.

Let's get started. If you've read this far, I know you're ready.

I am grateful you are here

Here's to loving yourself,

Christy

What is the MaxxMETHOD?

The MaxxMETHOD is a framework for personal development to help you build a foundation of self-worth and self-love through healing, increasing your emotional intelligence and self-mastery skills so you can manifest a life that excites you.

The word **METHOD** stands for:

- **M**indfulness: Learn a special kind of awareness that gets you results
- **E**motions: Engage with all of your emotions and feel more alive
- **T**houghts: Clear limiting beliefs and establish a helpful belief system
- **H**ealing: Heal your past and connect with your authentic self
- **O**wn Your Dreams: Discover new possibilities
- **D**o It NOW: Take action now

CHAPTER 1

Mindfulness

A Special Kind of Awareness

> "Awareness is the primary currency of
> the human condition."
> —Lama Surya Das, *Buddha Standard Time:
> Awakening to the Infinite Possibilities of Now*

In this chapter you will learn:

- The difference between mindfulness and awareness
- How awareness, acceptance, and understanding lead to healing and growth
- How to awaken to your life and quit living on autopilot
- That bringing significant matters into conscious awareness is powerful and life-changing
- How to face the storm with mindfulness
- That you can rewrite your story
- How to identify, face, and silence your inner critic
- How mindfulness helps cultivate self-compassion and re-bonding with who you are meant to be

Build the Foundation: Increase Self-Awareness, Acceptance, and Understanding

This workbook is not a mindfulness practice. It is a practice in loving yourself, and you cannot practice loving yourself without being mindful.

We cannot change anything until we first become
aware of what is, and with acceptance.

Mindfulness is a special kind of awareness whereby you learn to be aware of "what is" without any kind of judgment.

We're either aware of our misery and unhappiness and we judge the hell out of it and therefore, we want to ignore them in some way. Or, we're not aware at all.

Let's face it, most of the time we live on autopilot. I've worked with thousands of people in my therapy and coaching practice, and to some degree, each of them was living their life on autopilot. They were saying "yes" to things they didn't want to do and saying "no" to things they did want. They were tolerating things they didn't like and settling for mediocrity on so many levels.

Living on autopilot has enormous negative effects in many areas of our lives, most notably our relationships.

And, when I say relationships, I mean the relationship we have with ourselves, as well as the relationships we have with others.

We're disconnected from ourselves just as much as we're disconnected from our loved ones, and even in our supposedly most intimate relationships. We believe we need others in our lives because we think it will fill that void. We don't examine the void. We usually just keep living on autopilot, hoping it will all get better.

We white-knuckle it through our unhappiness and misery and hope things will change. We spend our days focusing on others, trying to get them to change so we can be happy. Simultaneously, we're chasing all kinds of things, people, gurus, and achievements hoping we'll find the secret to feeling better...to feel good enough...to believe we're lovable...so we can get rid of our anxiety, depression, anger, and other unpleasant emotions.

We do this all so automatically, we don't even know we're doing it. We are on autopilot, going through the motions and expecting outside sources to bring us happiness and love.

Well, I have news for you. Three things:

1. The most important relationship you will ever have is the one you have with yourself.
2. Developing self-love is an inside job. Nobody can do it for you.
3. This is your life and as far as I can tell, you have only one shot at it. Make it count.

So, here we are. You. Me. This workbook. And, your life.

If you're tired of where you are and you want to increase your self-worth, self-love, resilience, and become who you are meant to be, then you are in the right place. Now, you just have to do the work. The first step is awakening to you and your life. This is called mindfulness.

Once you increase your awareness with acceptance, you will develop a deeper understanding, all of which are catalysts to change, healing, and personal growth. This chapter is building the foundation for loving yourself and becoming who you are meant to be, and we all know how important it is to have a strong foundation.

Consequences of Lack of Mindfulness

Have you experienced any of the following recently? Check off all that apply:

- ❑ Lack of self-knowledge or confusion
- ❑ Repeating the same negative patterns
- ❑ Self-medicating with codependency, shopping, people-pleasing, drugs, alcohol, etc.
- ❑ Low self-worth, low self-esteem, lack of confidence
- ❑ Anxiety, depression, anger, insecurity, and other unpleasant emotions
- ❑ Inability to learn effective coping skills
- ❑ Difficulties in relationships
- ❑ Needing validation from others
- ❑ Not breaking the cycle of dysfunction
- ❑ Living small, not reaching your potential

If you've experienced any of these, you may be suffering from a lack of awareness and acceptance, or the uncertainty of how to change them. The first and most important step toward change is the practice of mindfulness.

What is Mindfulness?

Jon Kabat Zinn, the "father" of mindfulness, defines it as "paying attention in a particular way: on purpose, in the present moment, and nonjudgmentally."

Take a moment right now and notice your surroundings and internal experience. Tap into all five of your senses. What do you see? What colors stand out to you? What do you hear? Is there music? Sounds of family in the other room? What do you smell? The aroma of a good cup of coffee? Lasting hints of your favorite perfume? What do you taste? The afternotes of a quality glass of wine? Minty freshness of recently brushed teeth? What do you feel? Is your chair hard or soft? Are you comfortable in your clothes?

To live in the moment requires that you experience your moments to the fullest potential whenever possible and whenever necessary.

Mindfully focusing on your emotions, thoughts, dreams, wants, and desires will be the center of your awareness throughout this workbook and journal.

Mindfulness is necessary if you want to heal, grow, or transcend the negative effects of trauma, unpleasant emotions, grief and loss, or fear of getting out of your comfort zone. I'm not talking about a mindfulness practice of sitting for hours. I'm talking about increasing your awareness of your internal experience in your daily life.

Our natural tendency when we are feeling unpleasant emotions (e.g., anxiety, fear, hurt, envy), or experiencing unpleasant thoughts or beliefs (e.g., I am worthless, I'm not good enough, I can't have), is to avoid them at all costs. Unpleasant emotions and unpleasant thoughts are uncomfortable. Therefore, we develop ways to suppress, avoid, or self-medicate these thoughts and emotions with things such as work, busyness, alcohol, food, drugs, sex, or people-pleasing.

We try judging our uncomfortable emotions and negative thoughts as "bad" because we believe this will motivate us to change them. In actuality, these approaches do the opposite and keep us stuck in a vicious cycle of negativity.

Our poor maladaptive coping skills lead to more misery, lack of growth, problems in our relationships, and poor self-worth. Often, we are not even aware, mindful, or fully conscious of what we are doing. Sometimes we are aware, but we don't know how to make a change.

Facing the Storm

When suppressing, avoiding, and self-medicating stops working, our emotional pain comes to the forefront. We literally feel it in our bodies. We experience anxiety and shame as our stomachs churn. We feel a lack of motivation. We feel stuck and unsure of how to make those unpleasant emotions go away, which can lead us to feel the physical symptoms of depression or sadness. I call this "the storm" or "the darkness."

I describe this time as the way our body and mind tell us, "It's time to grow," or "It's time for change." If you use this time to become mindful and self-reflective, if you say, "YES!" to the storm and increase your level of awareness, you give yourself the opportunity to grow, evolve, and elevate your life.

When clients come to me, they are usually experiencing some kind of "storm." They have lots of anxiety, fear, sadness, anger, or other unpleasant emotions, which is usually a clue for me. They don't need a diagnosis—or medication—because the problem lies in a lack of self-understanding, lack of emotional intelligence, and unresolved pain.

Marlene came to me in the middle of a personal storm. Despite seeing a therapist for years and being on two different psychotropic medications for depression and anxiety, she was in a living hell and having regular panic attacks and anxiety every day. Her mind was racing with unpleasant and irrational thoughts that she felt she could not control.

She was desperate and ready for something to change.

As always, we first began by helping her become more mindful. She learned to increase her awareness and acceptance of her anxiety, sadness, and uncomfortable sensations in her body, as well as the many negative beliefs that were swirling in her mind all day long. She learned to no longer fight all of these unpleasant thoughts and feelings but instead invited them in with acceptance, comfort, and compassion.

Marlene was able to wean herself off all medications. She not only learned to cope much better with all the things that life threw at her, but she also learned to love herself and find greater joy in her life. Calmness and confidence replaced panic attacks. Self-love and a new zest for life replaced depression. To this day, she thanks me regularly for all the skills she learned and is able to use when life gets difficult or challenging.

Once we bring our experiences to the front of our consciousness with mindfulness, awareness, and deep understanding, we begin to naturally tap into our insight, wisdom, and openness. When we resource these, we make different choices, and we become more effective in establishing healthier psychological, emotional, and mental states.

You cannot change anything until you first pay attention purposefully in the present moment, and with acceptance rather than judgment. When we judge ourselves, we tend to focus on the negative aspects of things. This judgment is an important part of what keeps us stuck. With awareness and acceptance, you simply acknowledge the way things are (e.g., "I am sad, and that's my experience.") This is where progress begins.

Cultivate Self-Love Through Self-Acceptance

> "I just wanted someone to understand me, but what I didn't realize at the time was that that someone was me."
> —Rob Kish

When someone feels accepted in any kind of relationship, that person will become more of who he or she is meant to be. Acceptance and understanding breed motivation for transformation and growth. This is why the helping relationship is so important to personal change. I see it over and over again in my office. I can almost see each client sigh and relax when they realize they can be themselves. They will not be judged, criticized, or pathologized.

The first step is mindfulness, the next step is acceptance, and the result is understanding. Once people feel heard and seen for *who they are* in *any* relationship, their nervous system begins to relax. Wisdom begins transforming pain and regrets into healing and growth.

People will shrink in shame when criticized, judged, and neglected. This will not change unless they can see themselves with grace and understanding or if they're lucky enough to receive grace and understanding from a parent, teacher, coach, therapist, partner, or friend.

> *My belief is if we can cultivate that same level of acceptance and understanding with ourselves, we can self-heal, grow, and learn to love ourselves.*

You have picked up this workbook because you have come to a place in your life where you are feeling anxious, depressed, angry, unfulfilled, lonely, or even all of these at once. You know it's time for change. It's time for growth. Good for you for taking this courageous step into illuminating with mindfulness your negative thoughts and emotions and beginning the process of transforming your current state into more fulfilling relationships with yourself and others.

We all want more connection, love, joy, and success in our lives. When you complete the activities and *do the work* necessary, this workbook will help you achieve that.

All too often, we focus on the outside world to the detriment of the inside world. We believe it is what we *have* that will fill the void of our own emptiness. A relationship. A job. Approval from others. Degrees. Money. Appearances. Material things. Seeking worth from outside sources is a myth and does not result in true self-worth.

For lasting change to occur, you must first acknowledge your inside world and start the process there. Developing self-knowledge is how you develop true self-worth, learn to love yourself, and become who you are meant to be.

It will take a conscious effort and commitment on your part to move in the direction of self-discovery, healing, inner peace, confidence, and transformation. To start the process, it only takes a quiet space and ten minutes of your time.

MaxxExperience -
Silent Meditation Focusing on "What is"

You can learn to become more mindful with just ten minutes of silent meditation each day. Listen to what's going on internally: in your body, in your mind, and with your senses. Quieting your mind will help increase your awareness of your inner experience—your emotions, thoughts, and wants—so you can begin to learn how to better manage them. Set a timer for ten minutes. Allow yourself to sit or lie down in a comfortable seated or lying position. Close your eyes and focus on your breath.

If you notice your mind is wandering, just bring your focus back to your breath. When our minds are racing with thoughts, this is very difficult at first. Simply observe the thoughts, without judgment, and say to yourself things like "my mind is racing," "I'm aware of my racing thoughts," or simply "racing thoughts." And then focus on your breath by making statements to yourself such as "breathing in, breathing out."

The more you practice this, the better you're able to quiet those racing thoughts. This exercise is to help you slow down and listen.

Notice the various sensations in your body and perhaps in your mind. Perhaps you feel a tightness in your shoulders, a heaviness in your mind, or a jittery feeling in your stomach. Allow yourself to become mindful of your internal experience.

MaxxExperience -
Reflect and Write About Your Experience

- What did you notice about the sensations in your body?
- How would you describe these sensations?
- Did you feel any discomfort?
- Relaxed?
- Any pain?
- What did you notice about your thoughts?
- Did you become more aware of any certain emotion?
- If so, did you divert your attention, or did you focus on it?
- Did you notice any judgments that came up for you?

What's the Story You've Been Telling Yourself?

We all have a story we've made up about ourselves. Parts of our stories might be negative, and parts of our story might be positive. Most of the time, our stories of ourselves tend to be more negative. This exercise is the beginning of mindfulness and bringing your story into awareness so you can work on changing it—and finding the story you are meant to live!

MaxxExperience - What's Your Story?

Use this space to write the story you've been telling yourself about who you are.

What's the story you have been telling yourself? What are the limiting beliefs that make up your story? Limiting beliefs are thoughts that limit you in some way: *I can't, I'm not good enough, I shouldn't, I don't deserve love, I'm not worthy, I can't succeed.* How long have you been believing this story about yourself? When did you begin believing this story about yourself? How does this story affect your life? How does this story not serve you?

MaxxExperience - Write the Rest of Your Story!

Use this space to write your NEW story. Think about all the possibilities! Write the story you are meant to live! What is different in this story? What would you rather believe about yourself? How are you feeling in this story? How do you feel about yourself in this story? How do you see yourself in this story? How does this story change your life and your future? How does this story change you?

Mindfulness—Awakening to What YOU Want

We focus so much on others, we don't even know
ourselves and our wants, dreams, and desires.

Often, at the beginning of working with my clients, I ask them what they want. Most times they have no idea what they want, or their list is quite small. I believe we focus so much on others that we don't really know ourselves; as a result, we live small lives because we're not aware of what we want. You now get to become awakened to what YOU want. This is about you, your life, and your dreams.

What do you want in your life? In your relationships? In your career? One of my clients, John, was amazed at how much becoming more mindful opened up his world. He noticed how often he did not operate from a place of authenticity, especially in his relationship. He was often saying "yes" to things he had no desire to do. He was not communicating what he wanted, or didn't want, because he was not even aware of what he wanted or didn't want. He, like so many of us, was living on autopilot. He simply did not know what he did not know!

When he increased his level of awareness, he was much better at getting his own needs met, operating from a place of integrity, and as a result his relationship improved. He was able to work through resentment towards his wife that he had been holding on to for things he had never even asked for.

In order to become knowledgeable of who you are and what you want, you must increase your level of awareness. Think about the things you are saying "yes" to and really meaning "no," as well as the things you're saying "no" to and really meaning "yes."

Check out this article by Derek Sivers, from the book *Anything You Want*, 2006. What are you missing out on by not allowing yourself to say *Hell yeah!* or *Hell no!*?

MaxxExperience - What Do I Want?

*To get what you want out of your life,
you must first know what you want.*

It's time for you to stop the autopilot and increase your awareness of how you're living your life and what you're doing with it. I want you to think outside of the box and out of your comfort zone a bit. What would you do in your relationships if your heart was healed and open? What's the one crazy or secret idea you've always wanted to pursue? What would you do if you had unlimited money and time? What kind of people do you want in your circle? Who do you want to spend your time with? What do you most value and how can you share it with the world? What do you want to do as a way to give your life more meaning? What places do you want to see in your lifetime? If you were enjoying your life more, what would you do differently? If you didn't let fear stop you, what adventures would you want to participate in?

What do I want for myself?

Personally:

Relationships:

Health (Physical, Emotional, and Psychological Growth):

Professionally/Education:

Hobbies/Adventure/Fun:

MaxxExperience -
How Do I Limit or Stop Myself?

In getting the most out of my experience, what are some of the limiting beliefs about my story and habits that are holding me back?

Personally:

Relationships:

Health (Physical, Emotional, and Psychological Growth):

Professionally/Education:

Hobbies/Adventure/Fun:

Facing Your Inner Critic

Remember, mindfulness is awareness **without judgment**. By judgment, I mean harsh criticism of yourself. This is very different from discernment, which is when you make a conscious, and helpful, evaluation of yourself. You can discern that you made a mistake and feel badly, apologetic, or even guilty. However, it's not necessary to react harshly with self-loathing and criticism. And, most importantly it's not helpful.

The first step is awareness. The second step is acceptance. This is where you will begin to face your inner critic and the judgments you place on yourself.

> "If you give your inner genius as much
> credence as your inner critic,
> you would be light years ahead of
> where you now stand."
> —Alan Cohen

Consequences of the Inner Critic

Have you experienced any of the following? Check off all that apply:

- ❑ Anxiety
- ❑ Insecurity
- ❑ Self-Doubt
- ❑ Depression
- ❑ Living Small
- ❑ Low Self-Worth
- ❑ Relationship Issues

☐ Lack of Confidence
☐ Self-Medicating/Addictions
☐ People Pleasing/Codependency

If you've experienced any of these, there's a good chance you may be suffering from an inner critic.

Where Does the Inner Critic Come From?

We live in a world where criticizing and disciplining have been used to modify behavior. However, it does not work. Criticism was modeled to us during childhood from parents, caretakers, teachers, and society. We learn that it's easier to create and believe a false, negative belief than it is to believe a more positive belief. Self-criticism becomes habitual, and we often don't even notice we're doing it.

Being Critical Does *Not* Work

- Inner Critic = Victim Mentality = Helpless/Hopeless
- I cannot make myself happy
- Other people are responsible for my happiness
- I am powerless over how I feel and what happens to me
- Other people's feelings are more important than mine
- If someone is upset, it's my fault
- I cannot handle the emotional pain and/or it will never end
- To feel emotional pain is weak, so I'll bury it
- Taking care of myself and making myself happy is selfish

Recent research is discovering that being judgmental does not work. Self-compassion and self-kindness are what create greater change and transformation. For a more in-depth study of self-compassion, see Kristen Neff's book, *Self-Compassion: The Proven Power of Being Kind to Yourself.*

Rewards of Cultivating Self-Compassion

- More confidence
- Stronger sense of self, self-worth, and self-esteem
- Mental and physical well-being
- Resilience
- Healthier relationships
- Ability to assert yourself and implement healthier boundaries
- Increased level of happiness and well-being
- Greater levels of success, purpose, and meaning in your life

> *The most important relationship you will ever have*
> *is the relationship you have with yourself.*
> *Talk to yourself as you would a good friend.*

The Three Types of Inner Critics (Adapted from Healing Your Aloneness by Erika J. Chopich and Margaret Paul)

- The Compliant
- The Controlling
- The Resistor

Often, we have a combination of all three.

The **compliant** believes she is responsible for other people's happiness and unhappiness. She believes she gets her self-worth and love from others by taking care of them. She believes it's easier to give in than to have an argument.

An example of the compliant would be Melinda, a 50-year-old woman, who called me crying because her life felt so out of control. She was drinking heavily. Her husband and three daughters were disappointed and no longer trusted her. Today, she still laughs because she called me three times sobbing uncontrollably before she actually made an appointment. As fearful and miserable as she was, she knew she wanted change and she took the courageous step toward investing in herself.

In our work together, she discovered that she was an extreme people pleaser, and it had taken its toll. She learned this behavior as a child while growing up with parents who were using drugs, didn't work, and neglected many of her needs. As a result, Melinda became "parentified," and learned to care for her parents and siblings, possibly in hopes that she would receive attention and love in return.

Years of people-pleasing emptied her emotional tank, and as a result, she lacked self-worth, lost her voice, had difficulty making decisions, was unhappy, and ended up self-medicating with alcohol.

After facing and healing her inner critic, she no longer drank, her relationships with her husband and daughters were healing quickly, and she began her journey of genuine self-love and self-worth. Since our work together, she has traveled to Europe (something she would never have done due to extreme anxiety) and even went to Italy, where she had only one glass of wine! She is now working outside of the home and texts me regularly, telling me how she's a different person. It's such a joy to hear the happiness in her voice!

The second type, the **controlling** inner critic, is very judgmental of other people and very critical of herself as well. She is angry, negative, and dominant. She believes the way to get love is to demand it. An example of this would be Patricia.

Patricia came to me because of an estranged relationship with her only daughter. Her daughter refused to talk to her and cut her out of her life. She was extremely guarded and blamed everything on her ex-husband and her "difficult" daughter.

Though she was harsh and critical of herself, she could not see that she was playing a part in pushing her daughter away. After digging a bit into her past, she admitted that as a child, she often longed for affection from her depressed mom and secretly hated her dad for being strict and critical.

She modeled her unavailable mom and critical father and after several years she felt alone and lost.

She began to see her own negative, critical, and demanding traits, and this was when her heart began to soften. Once she understood her own vulnerability and her desire for love, she no longer felt the need to demand it from her daughter. Her negative self-talk decreased, and the walls began to come down.

The **resistor** is the one who avoids interactions, self-medicates, usually feels indifferent, dead, and numb, and avoids self-responsibility. She believes she doesn't deserve love, so why even bother? She's rebellious. She believes she is permanently damaged because that's what's been projected onto her.

Lisa struggled with neglect and abuse from an early age. She came to me feeling so depressed and anxious that she often felt numb. She drank as a way to self-medicate her pain and ignore what was really going on with her.

Her inner critic was rebellious, extremely self-critical, and didn't care about herself at all. She believed she was permanently damaged.

Working at a pace set by her, layer by layer, we began to peel away the suffering and pain she had been carrying. We did this in group and in individual coaching. Brick by brick, I watched as she began building a foundation of true self-worth. As a result, she began setting healthy boundaries, and her negative self-statements began decreasing. She began smiling and enjoying her life again.

Where Does Your Inner Critic Come From?

- Our inner critics come from messages we make up about ourselves as a response to our experiences and environment.
- If someone hurts us, neglects our needs, or traumatizes us, we respond by creating a negative inner dialogue.
- We learn to abandon ourselves and even stop loving ourselves.
- We repeat what we see in our parents, siblings, teachers, and other caregivers when they model unloving, unkind, or critical behavior toward themselves, ourselves, or others.
- We learn to be hard on ourselves as a coping mechanism.

MaxxExperience -
Getting to Know Your Inner Critic

Identify at what age you began being critical of yourself. Write about all the ways you learned to abandon yourself. Describe the ways in which you began unloving behavior toward yourself and all the ways you became self-critical.

MaxxExperience -
4-Steps to Silence Your Inner Critic

1. **Mindfulness:** How often does negative self-talk happen? What are the consequences of your inner critic? What are the typical negative self-talk conversations that occur for you? Be mindful of the inner critic in your day-to-day activities.

2. **Acceptance/Understanding:** Judging your critic will not help it go away. Use the power of acceptance. Say things like, "This is my critic, and I will curiously investigate where it came from." "This is my critic, and I'm getting to know that part of myself. I also want to get to know the part of myself who wants to have more self-love and self-kindness." Convey an understanding of how the inner critic was developed and your desire to be more kind and loving toward yourself.

3. **Choice:** You are now bringing the inner critic into the conscious, into your awareness. When you bring things into your awareness, you have an opportunity to make a choice. Do I want to keep talking to myself in this way? What do I want for myself and my life? Write about the choices you want to make starting now.

4. **Practice:** Do something different. Practice more loving or gentle behavior. How would you speak to a friend

if they were in the same situation? Practice, practice, practice. Write some ways you can speak more kindly to yourself. Describe your life without the inner critic.

Learning Self-Compassion Through Reparenting and Rebonding

> "Reach deep inside until you find the
> unworthiness that has always been there.
> Hold it until it cries. It has been waiting to be held,
> loved and seen by you. Only you."
> —Unknown

Imagine yourself when you were five years old, ten, or even eighteen. What does she look like? What is she wearing? Is her hair long, short, or in pigtails? What does her smile look like? Imagine what it's like being her. Imagine holding her.

Welcome to your "inner child." And, most times, she is your "wounded inner child." Our "wounded inner child" is the one we unintentionally abandoned. The one who made up negative beliefs about herself. The one who needs your love and compassion.

It's time for you to reparent her/him because that is your authentic self. That is where your self-worth is, for she was born worthy. "Reparenting" is a way to go back to your "wounded inner child" and begin the journey of uncovering your authentic self.

As children, we are influenced by our experiences and environment. Even in the best of households and the best of parenting, we sometimes construct negative messages about ourselves. We learn to devalue ourselves in our schools, with certain teachers or peers. Sometimes, how we learn to devalue ourselves depends on our temperament. What might negatively affect one sibling or student may not phase another. We are also affected according to our "thinking style," such as pessimistic or optimistic.

I was lucky enough to learn early on how my thinking could have such an impact on my emotions, my self-worth, self-esteem, and my life in general.

When I was in high school, I remember a time we had a car wash, and Mr. Campbell, the teacher in charge, became angry with someone and grabbed a bucket out of my hand somewhat aggressively. The bucket ended up cutting my finger. Not only was my finger hurt, but my feelings were also hurt. I remembered thinking such thoughts as, *he must not like me and this must mean I deserved this in some way because of who I am; This must be about me—that I'm not good enough in some way.* I was hurt for a couple of days and feeling really down. I didn't like how I felt and the road I was taking, and began rethinking, *He was angry at someone else, not me; It had nothing to do with me,* and *He must have a short fuse, which really has nothing to do with me.*

I vividly remember the change in my mood, in the way I saw myself. I knew I was destined to help others do the same.

The focus of this work is never to blame, but to help you become more authentic with how you responded to your experiences. In order to rediscover our authenticity we must dig into parts of our past to see how we've abandoned our own authentic selves. This is where healing begins so that you can uncover all the ways in which you are hindering your own self-worth and self-love.

We do this as adults, also. It's part of human nature.
We are meant to belong, and we want to belong;
therefore, we will abandon our true selves
in order to conform and fit in.

Reparenting is a very powerful and effective way of giving your "inner child" the nurturing and compassion she did not receive as a child. These types of rebonding exercises bring you back to your true self. By using experiential exercises, you can help heal your inner child from the negative messages and negative inner dialogue you adopted about yourself and get back to your true self-worth.

I also see reparenting as a way of rebonding with yourself so you can create a secure and safe attachment with yourself, which will also contribute to the health of your relationships with others. When you begin to have a deeper understanding, with acceptance, of how you got to where you are, you will notice transformation, change, and personal growth.

Remember, the most important relationship you have
is the relationship you have with yourself.
Let's create a healthy, secure relationship!

MaxxExperience -
Letter from Your Inner Child

If your younger self (your inner child) felt free to tell the adults in her life exactly what she needed, wanted, felt, and thought, what would she say? Think of what age your inner critic began and speak from your younger self at that age. Allow yourself to write about how she is feeling and what it's like to be her. Write about her emotions, thoughts, wants, and dreams. Write freely with no need to censor. Sometimes it helps to get a photo of yourself as a child. Access this photo anytime you want to begin understanding your inner child.

Dear Mom/Dad/Caregiver,

MaxxExperience -
Letter of Kindness from Your Inner Parent

Reparent with acceptance and understanding.
Begin building the healing relationship
with your inner child.

Now *you* get to be your own parent. This is where you get to re-bond with yourself through connecting your inner child and inner parent. We learn to judge ourselves so much that it becomes habitual. To make changes, you must practice kinder, more compassionate self-talk, even if it doesn't feel true at first. Believe me, at first, it will feel much like a foreign language. By the end of this workbook, you will feel more natural at it, and it will feel more authentic.

In response to the letter written above, write a compassionate letter to your inner child. If you have difficulty, pretend you are writing to your own child or a friend's child. Believing and feeling the self-compassion you are worthy of comes with practice. Use this space to write to your younger self all the things she needed to hear. Tell her you see and hear her and that you want to gain a deeper understanding of her. Write freely and without editing.

Dear <u>Younger Self,</u>

RECAP: How to Be Mindful, Increasing Awareness With Acceptance

- Short, quiet meditations to increase awareness of internal experiences to awaken yourself.
- Begin increasing your awareness (by noticing and observing) your emotions, thoughts, wants, and struggles. This is the beginning of change and transformation.
- Set intentions for yourself. Become more aware of how you're living on autopilot. Be okay with saying "no" to things you don't want to do.
- Be more mindful of your inner critic. With awareness you now have a choice.
- Increase self-kindness and begin reparenting your inner child with compassion and kindness. Rebond with younger adult versions of yourself also.
- Practice, practice, practice mindfulness.

CHAPTER 2

Emotions

Finding Resilience and Balance

"The best and most beautiful things in the
world cannot be seen or even touched.
They must be felt with the heart."
—Helen Keller

In this chapter you will learn:

- How we learn to devalue our emotions
- The unhelpful messages you adopted as a child regarding your emotions and how to change them
- The importance of your emotions, how to feel and manage them
- The power of self-compassion as a healing technique and a way to true self-worth and self-love
- How to use your breath to comfort unpleasant emotions
- The importance of laughter and experiencing pleasant emotions

Emotion

Lexico.com says an emotion is "A NATURAL instinctive state of mind deriving from one's circumstances, mood, or relationships with others. Emotions are a normal human response.

How We Learn to Devalue Our Emotions

I knew as a child that emotions were important. I also knew that nurturing each other and ourselves was essential to the human process. I guess you could say I had a natural emotional intelligence in many ways.

> *Unfortunately, we come from an*
> *emotionally neglectful society.*

In my family, our feelings were sometimes talked about, and sometimes they were not. Sometimes they were nurtured, and sometimes they were not. It seemed, most times, nobody ever talked about their feelings. Not in schools. Not in our churches. Not with my friends or their families.

Many clients come to me, and they don't want to blame their parents. Most will say, "My parents were great parents." Unfortunately, therapy has gained a reputation for blaming our childhoods and parents for "all" issues that we experience in our adulthood. I met a man at a party this week who said, "I just don't like therapy because my parents didn't do anything wrong, and therapy always blames the parents. My parents did the best they could."

I would like to clarify some things. First, this workbook and the work I do with my clients is never about blame. It's about finding out how we responded to our childhood and how our past (even our past as adults) still affects us now!

Parenting can be difficult, especially when most parents have no idea what emotional intelligence is, how to heal their own past wounds, or have no idea of how to get help or how to learn the tools necessary to parent in the best way possible.

Some parents are mildly neglectful and punitive despite good intentions and deep love for their children. Others are grossly neglectful and abusive and have no shame for what they do. This also goes for any caretaker, teacher, clergy, or adult in a child's life.

The other factor involves how we respond as children. One child may feel ignored and unloved, while another in the same family may feel a sense of belonging. One child may be traumatized by a certain experience, and their sibling may be able to let it roll off their back, leaving no ill effects.

Trauma and how we respond to our past and our childhood is a very individual experience. Trauma also occurs in adulthood. All traumas (mild and severe) are valid and worthy of being heard, seen, and healed.

We All Want to Be Seen and Heard

If we are able to see and hear ourselves, we will be better at seeing and hearing our loved ones. This is what will break cycles of abuse and trauma.

As I have said above, we also have unresolved issues from our adult lives. I have clients come into my office because they never fully grieved or healed from a loved one's death that occurred ten years prior. I've been through the loss of four great friends—one being my sister, as I spoke about in the introduction. I've had adult relationships that ended in relatively traumatic ways.

My point is, the peaks and valleys of life continue into our adulthood; yet most of us don't have the tools and skills to grieve, to heal, and to cope with the normal human experience that we all go through. We sometimes end up coping as we did in childhood.

The good news is, now you can take control, heal your past once and for all, become more emotionally resilient, and become who you are meant to be!

You Can Run But You Cannot Hide

It's no wonder many of us are afraid to feel our emotions. We've never been taught to feel them. We're taught quite the opposite. Ignore them. Squelch them. Avoid them. Suppress them. DO NOT talk about them.

In fact, we are all emotional beings. If you are human, you were born with a limbic system, which means you have emotions. We feel many of our emotions physically in our bodies, and some emotions can be enormously painful.

You may have learned early on to adopt a strategy to avoid feeling that physical, emotional pain. For some, that strategy can work for their entire life.

When we learn to repress our unpleasant emotions,
we are likely repressing our pleasant emotions also.

When we repress, avoid, deny, or self-medicate our emotions, we are living as inauthentic people. We are not allowing our full, complete, authentic selves to exist.

In completing this workbook, you will begin to embrace the whole of your being. It won't be easy. You may feel enormous physical pain when you allow your repressed sorrow to come to the forefront, or when you face the shame that has been buried within you for years.

Let me warn you: It will hurt physically in your body, but it's like strengthening a muscle. When you practice comforting your unpleasant emotions, it will get easier, and you will become more proficient at it.

Consequences of Not Mastering Your Emotions

Are you experiencing any of the following? Check all that apply:

- ❑ Unpleasant emotions are left unresolved
- ❑ Lacking a sense of an emotional foundation
- ❑ Unaware of how to handle normal human emotions
- ❑ Emotional immaturity
- ❑ Intense and more frequent unpleasant emotions
- ❑ Shutting off an emotional part of yourself; feeling numb
- ❑ Self-medicating with drugs, alcohol, shopping, food, sex, etc.
- ❑ Not experiencing pleasant emotions—love, joy, excitement, trust
- ❑ Staying in victim stance

> "That breath that you just took, that's a gift!"
> —Robert Bell

MaxxExperience - Breathing Meditation

Your breath alone can be enormously healing for your unpleasant emotions. Try it right now. Think of something that may be slightly frustrating or stressful for you right now. Begin breathing and become aware of where you feel the sensation of that stress or frustration in your body. Now, breathe into it. Breathe in and breathe out. Do this six to eight times and notice any changes. It's likely that you felt the intensity of the stress or frustration decrease.

The more you allow your breath to nurture your pain, the more adept you become at managing this part of your being. The more you allow yourself to embrace your challenging emotions, the more you experience the whole spectrum of emotions on a grand scale. The more you experience your challenging emotions, the more resilient you become with the ups and downs of life. You will notice unpleasant emotions decreasing in frequency and intensity, and pleasant emotions increasing. It doesn't happen overnight; it takes time, and it takes practice.

Jessica came to me with such severe anxiety from a long history of trauma. She had recently been diagnosed with conversion disorder and put on disability. She literally would just think of her mom and immediately have a seizure. She practiced breathing and other effective techniques, and within just a matter of weeks, she was much more able to be in control of her anxiety rather than her anxiety controlling her.

After the deep work regarding her own trauma and allowing her emotions with mindfulness, she is now experiencing greater joy and happiness in many aspects of her life. She was even able to return to work.

There has been much research these days on the importance and effectiveness of emotional intelligence skills and training to be a more effective leader in the workplace. My hope is that this trend continues into the mainstream population to help increase mental, emotional, and psychological health.

We are taught to invalidate our emotions, ignore or judge them, which inhibits our ability to process emotions in a healthy way.

When we do this, we cut off our driving force. If we become more intelligent in our own emotional being, we can then become more intelligent in how we interact in our relationships with ourselves and with others.

> *One of the most important times for*
> *self-love, self-care, and self-compassion*
> *is when you are suffering.*

When I went through my struggles that led me to create this workbook, I was grieving. There was so much chaos, tragedy, and loss going on in my life that I self-medicated with being busy. With work. With friends. With anything I could do to distract myself. I continued until I realized I was hurting internally, and my body was paying the price.

Once I began the work on myself, my body was not well. I had a terrible case of insomnia on top of everything. I didn't even have the energy to sit while meditating. I listened to my body and I knew I needed to lie down. I needed something that would feel comfortable, comforting, and healing.

Each morning I would lay on the floor with a pillow under my chest and head with arms to my side and heart open; and I allowed myself to lie there simply focusing on my breath and my body. Quietly. With no intention whatsoever except to rest with my breath. I began to become aware of all the sensations I was feeling. I noticed areas where I stored my stress. I discovered where I hid my grief. I felt every ounce of my pain and I allowed my breath to begin the healing process of acceptance. I had to accept where I was in order to move forward. And, I had to do it gently.

MaxxExperience -
Meditation: Embracing Your Suffering Self

Now it's your turn to begin embracing all of who you are. I recommend this exercise, especially when you're struggling with very painful emotions, insomnia, or exhaustion. Lie down on the floor with a pillow underneath, from the top of your head to your lower back. Allow your arms to drop to each side, with your heart open.

Have no intention other than to rest and use your breath to begin healing yourself. You may begin to notice an increased awareness of all the sensations of your body. Where do you hold stress? What emotions feel the strongest? What emotions are you hiding from? Allow yourself to cry. To sob. Whatever you need. Breathe in deeply and breathe out, allowing each breath to move into the sensation you're focusing on and then releasing. Do this for at least 20 minutes. Set a timer if that helps.

You can do this exercise by focusing on one emotion at a time if that feels more comfortable for you. I do suggest you do this exercise daily, until you feel the emotions moving on, or until your body feels more rested.

The Human Experience and Human Connection

Reaching out for support and connection in
our human experience is vital to our existence.
We are all in this together.

It's not only okay to not be okay, it also okay to reach out for support. I'm going to go one step further and say it's healthy to reach out for help and support. We are meant for connection, to help each other, and to nurture each other. When I talk of self-love, it doesn't mean you're to do it alone. Not at all. If anything, it will help you reach out in healthier ways. We need one another.

I have many memories of my loved ones being there for me. One of the most memorable moments was with my dad when I was grieving a relationship. My dad came to help me move and he saw the tears in my eyes and he just hugged me. He didn't say anything. He didn't have to. That hug was all I needed to help me get through that moment, that day, that experience.

I've never been shy about reaching out to my closest friends and family when I'm struggling or experiencing any kind of difficulty. I reach out to the ones who I know won't judge me, who will listen, who will support me no matter what, who will comfort me, challenge me, and who will make me laugh.

MaxxExperience - Connecting to Others

Think of the people in your life and begin making a list of those you can reach out to. Who will challenge you? Who will comfort you? Who will accept you where you're at? Who will make you laugh? Who will join you in working through the MaxxMETHOD Workbook?

1.
2.
3.
4.
5.

Part of self-knowledge is knowing what you need,
who you need, and when you need it.

My hope for you is that you learn to recognize your full spectrum of emotions, cope with these emotions, and express them in ways that help build resilience. You will also find that by allowing yourself to integrate your emotions with compassion, you will see things differently, with clarity, in color, and with more positivity. You will build confidence in yourself and your ability to get through the things that life throws your way.

You'll notice that you're feeling fewer unpleasant emotions and more pleasant emotions. You'll feel a sense of strength, even if you're feeling sad. You'll no longer buy into unhelpful myths such as "crying is weak," "men shouldn't be vulnerable," or "I'm emotional so I must be crazy."

Let's get started. Let's get to know the emotional parts of you and learn to embrace them!

Basic emotions

1. Joy
2. Fear
3. Guilt
4. Love
5. Trust
6. Anger
7. Shame
8. Sadness/Grief
9. Remorse/Regret

We live in an emotionally neglectful society.

What kind of messages about emotions did you adopt from your childhood, society, peers, parents, teachers, or clergy?

- Crying is weak.
- Emotions are bad.
- If you're upset, I won't love you, or I'll be angry with you.
- It's best to just keep them to yourself; nobody talks about them.
- It's not okay to feel or show your emotions.
- Men can't cry, or boys don't cry.
- Feelings are stupid.
- Don't be a crybaby.
- You can't handle anything.
- It's not okay to be unhappy, so you should fake it.
- You're overly dramatic.
- As a man, the only emotion that's okay is anger.
- Women are too emotional.
- Women are weak.
- Anger is bad.
- You can't handle your emotions.

"Unprocessed emotions will never die.
They are buried alive and will come forth in uglier ways."
—Sigmund Freud

MaxxExperience -
Childhood Messages About Emotions

Become mindful of these messages and bring them into your awareness. Write five messages you learned as a child:

1.

2.

3.

4.

5.

MaxxExperience -
What Childhood Messages Are You *Still* Believing and Holding On To?

Become mindful of these messages and bring them into your awareness. Write five messages you continue to believe about your emotions and your emotional self:

1.

2.

3.

4.

5.

As a child, what did you need to learn about your emotions?

- Your emotions are important, and they are part of who you are.
- You can come and talk to me about what you're feeling.
- You can learn to manage your emotions.
- Having emotions is normal.
- There's nothing wrong with you.
- Emotions will come and go.
- Emotions are messages, and you can learn to listen to them.
- I will love you no matter what emotions you experience or how you manage them.
- I will have compassion for you when you feel _____, and you can learn to have compassion for yourself.

*You now get to decide how you
want to see your emotions.*

One of the most healing and transformative moments in my own personal therapy was when I went to a Gestalt therapist for the first time prior to starting my psychotherapy private practice. I was explaining my sadness or pain over a situation, and he instructed me to say, "I'm feeling my sadness, and that's my experience."

I was almost shocked. It was the first time someone, outside my family, had validated my feelings so completely and encouraged *me* to validate my own feelings. Ha, what a concept! Until then, I felt as if I was living in an emotionally neglectful society. Accepting and actually experiencing the emotion (versus just talking about) is healing and transformative! That experience helped me embrace all of myself and helped me feel more authentic with myself. My Gestalt therapist allowed, encouraged, and accepted the emotional part of me, which taught me to do the same for myself.

This experience contributed to my decision to continue with a three-year Gestalt training and has been a significant piece of my work with my clients.

Honoring our truth about our emotions
is one of the most powerful ways to
move through our emotions.

MaxxExperience -
Identify five statements you want to believe about
your emotions and your emotional self.

1.

2.

3.

4.

5.

What Is Your Emotional Intelligence?

Emotional intelligence is:

- The ability to be aware of, manage, and express one's emotions.
- The ability to be aware of, manage, and express one's own thoughts.
- The ability to understand another's emotional experience and perspective.
- The ability to have empathy for another's situation.
- The ability to handle interpersonal relationships more effectively.

MaxxExperience - Quiz - What is your emotional intelligence? Scale each sentence on a scale of 0 to 10 (10 is proficient).

_____ 1. I am very aware of my emotions and what is triggering them.

_____2. I am aware of the sensations in my body that are associated with each emotion.

_____3. I know which thoughts I have that are irrational or self-defeating and not serving me.

_____4. I am able to change my self-defeating irrational thoughts.

_____5. I am able to have self-compassion and soothe my unpleasant emotions.

_____6. I am able to freely express how I feel.

_____7. I can understand when someone else may be experiencing unpleasant emotions, and I easily have empathy for them.

_____8. I am able to resolve conflicts with others.

_____9. I am able to listen to others.

_____10. I am able to understand that other people may have a different perspective than I do.

_____Total

- **Stage 1:** 0–20 You will benefit greatly from learning more about emotional intelligence skills to help you in all areas of your life.
- **Stage 2:** 21–40 You are at the beginning of understanding your emotions, thoughts, wants, and desires, and how these affect the relationship with yourself, others, and your life.
- **Stage 3:** 41–60 You are on your way to becoming an emotionally intelligent person, which is beginning to

show in your relationships, your self-worth, and how you live your life.

- **Stage 4:** 61–80 You continue to progress above average in emotional intelligence.
- **Stage 5:** 81–100 Congratulations, you are on the high end of emotional intelligence and it shows in your emotional resilience and your relationship with others.

> "Have a sense of gratitude for everything,
> even difficult emotions, because of their
> potential to wake you up."
> —Pema Chodron

Emotions are energy, and they show up in our bodies as sensations: tingling, heaviness, tightness, warmth, jitters, a dull ache, physical pain, and contracting muscles, just to name a few. These are sensations that you actually feel in your body.

Emotions are also messages. Learn to listen to them. They carry important messages about your needs.

Emotions belong to *you*. They are yours. It's important that you own and take responsibility for your emotions. They reside in your body, your mind, your limbic system. Get rid of "victim" language, such as "she made me feel angry." When you use this language, you are giving someone else power over your own emotions.

Empower yourself, even in your language
by taking responsibility for how you feel.

For example, "I felt so angry when she _____,"
"I feel sad when he _____."

Anger (irritation, frustration, resentment)

- Anger tells us that a personal boundary may be violated.
- There are often more vulnerable emotions under the anger (sadness, jealousy). This is usually the result of accumulated unresolved issues from the past that are not being addressed. Our bodies have a way of talking to us, so it's important to listen.
- Anger usually shows up as sensations in our fists, feet, jaw, neck, or stomach. It may feel like a sense of power or intense energy, pressure, or rage.

Grief

What I learned in my experience of
losing my sister is that grief is truly about love.

Someone once said to me "you can still love your sister, even when she's gone." After feeling the pain, I noticed something shifting. Each time that wave of pain came over me, I allowed myself to also feel the love I have for her. Not only did my love for her grow, my pain lessened, and my heart opened. I don't miss her any less. I think of her often and wish we could go shopping and have lunch just one more time, but it always comes with an intense love for her and appreciation that I had her in my life.

Sadness/Grief (lonely, hurt, pity)

- Sadness tells us we've been hurt or are experiencing a loss.
- Sometimes sadness can turn into depression if not addressed.

- Sadness shows up as sensations in our stomach, heart/chest, face/eyes, and mouth.

Fear (apprehensive, cautious, threatened, overwhelmed)

- Fear tells us to lead with caution.
- We allow fear to keep us in our comfort zones (fear of failure/success).
- Irrational fear can lead to anxiety.
- Again, some anxiety is our body's way of telling us we have unresolved issues or are not living up to our potential. *I see this often.*
- Fears show up as sensations in our stomach (butterflies), a jittery feeling throughout our limbs, or sometimes as a feeling of our heart dropping into our stomachs.

Guilt (regretful, remorseful)

- Guilt tell us we made a mistake. It keeps us in check.
- Guilt shows up as a gnawing sensation.
- Sometimes guilt is useless ("I'm selfish if I take time for myself").

Shame can be extremely toxic

- Shame can be guilt carried too far. Making a mistake or having regrets and carrying the guilt for years is toxic.
- It says, "I'm a bad person" and "I'm worthless."
- Blaming yourself for something you didn't do.
- Sometimes we carry someone else's shame, especially when they have no shame. You may be carrying the shame that belongs to the person who DID do something shameful.

- Shame usually shows up as a sensation deep in the solar plexus (in the pit of the stomach).

Joy (hopeful, happy, excited, elated)

- Joy tells us things are great with our world.
- Joy shows up as a lightness throughout the body. All is well with the world.

Love (affection, compassion, warmth)

- Love tells us we are valued, important, and wanted. This includes self-love.
- Love tells us we are secure.
- Love shows up as warmth and swelling sensations in the chest area.
- The more we love ourselves, the better we feel about ourselves.
- When we receive love from others, it fuels our self-worth as well.
- Often, love is mistaken with infatuation or the fantasy stage of a relationship.

Trust (confidence, reliability, comfort)

- Trust tells us we can depend on ourselves or another. With trust, we have faith in ourselves or in another person.
- Trust show up as confidence that we can handle what comes our way or we can rely on another to be there for us.
- Trust is a belief in the goodness of others and in the ability of yourself to make good judgments.

Emotions Show up in Your Body

In my Gestalt therapy training, very early in my career, we were taught the importance of watching our client's body language. Sometimes it's apparent how a client is feeling just by watching their body language. This next exercise will help you become more aware of your emotions and how they show up in your body. We are used to *not* feeling our emotions, therefore, when you begin this work it may be somewhat uncomfortable. Remember, your breath can help comfort and alleviate the sensations of each emotion. The more you practice the easier it gets.

Sensations. Tense, tight, clenched, sweaty, dull, achy, calm, energized, jittery, warm, hot, cool, light, spacious, thick, blocked, disconnected, numb, empty, constricted, open, relaxed, heavy, hollow, nauseous, shaky, trembling, twitchy, draining, expanding. You may come up with some of your own sensations.

Scaling. Sometimes it helps to measure your emotion on a scale of 0/10—this will give you a sense of how intense your emotions are and how your emotions can decrease as you learn to care for them.

MaxxExperience - Getting To Know Your Emotions

Sit quietly and close your eyes. Increase your awareness of your internal experience. Using the list of possible sensations, notice any tight areas, open space, jittery sensations, warm sensations, dull aches, heaviness, etc. Emotions are measured on a scale of 0 to 10 (0 = nothing, 10 = extreme). Measure each emotion as you go through this exercise on a scale of 0/10.

Emotion	Body—Where do you feel the emotion?	Sensation	Scale 0/10
Sadness (example)	my heart, my eyes	an ache in my heart, tearful	7/10
Sadness			
Anger			
Fear			
Anxiety			
Shame			
Guilt			
Joy			
Love			

You can come back to the above exercise at any time when you're experiencing any emotion. Once you have become more aware of how your emotions are showing up in your body, you can then learn how to care for them using the following MaxxExperience.

MaxxExperience -
4 Steps to Caring for Your Emotions Using the
Acronym MAKE

MAKE a powerful decision to care for your emotions, so you no longer have to repress them. There are four steps to changing the habit of avoiding your emotions and then practice being kind and loving to yourself through those emotions. Emotions come and go. Always remember this when you're feeling intense, unpleasant emotions such as loneliness or grief. Tomorrow will be a new day, and your mood may be completely different. Emotions are a part of who you are. Once you learn to embody them with acceptance, you will allow a fuller expression of yourself.

1. **Mindfulness:** Be aware of the emotion. Discover the sensation. Where does it show up in your body?
2. **Acceptance:** Label it. Accept it by saying, "I'm feeling my sadness, and it's okay."
3. **Kindness:** Be kind to yourself. Breathe in comfort, breathe out judgment. Allow the breath to move into that area in your body where you're experiencing the sensation of that emotion. Breathe in compassion, breathe out negativity or criticism. What kinds of things might you say, or do, to a friend if they were struggling? Say and do those things to yourself. Put your hand on your heart if you are grieving or sad.
4. **Expression:** Forms of expression can be writing letters (for yourself), journaling, drawing, visualization, listening to music, dancing, or meditation.

MaxxExperience -
Write Three Unpleasant Emotions You Can Face, Comfort, and Care For This Week

1.

2.

3.

MaxxExperience -
Write the MAKE 4-step process for managing these unpleasant emotions.

This exercise will help you build emotional resilience, which leads to self-worth, confidence, and more effective coping skills. Emotions can be measured on a scale of 0 to 10 (0 = nothing, 10 = extreme). Scale each emotion in the first step (Mindfulness) and after the last step (Expression) so you can notice any changes.

1. **Mindfulness**: What emotion are you feeling? Where does it show up in your body? How would you describe the sensation? On a scale of 0-10, how uncomfortable is the emotion: _____0/10

2. **Acceptance:** Labeling the emotion is important. It gives a sense of acceptance. "I'm feeling my _____ and that's my experience."

"I'm feeling my _____ and it's okay."

"I'm feeling my _____ and I can handle it."

"I'm feeling my _____ and I still love myself."

"I'm feeling my _____ and _____."

3. **Kindness:** Be kind to yourself and use your breath to comfort this emotion. Allow yourself to breathe into the sensations of that emotion in your body. Breathe in comfort, breathe out judgment. Do this for at least six breaths. Write about your experience. Did the emotion subside or become less intense? If not, try breathing into the emotion/sensation in your body again six to eight times.

4. **Expression:** Use drawing, journaling, letter writing, etc., to express your emotion. Write or draw about how you're feeling. Write a letter to that emotion (Dear Anger...)

(blank box)

Now measure your emotion (0 = nothing, 10 = extreme): _____0/10. Great job! Hopefully you were able to comfort and work _through_ the emotion, rather than resist it.

Nicole came to me with an anger problem. She thought she had forgiven and let go of issues related to an absent father who abandoned her mother and siblings at such a young age. Her anger had become her coping mechanism. In some ways, it felt less painful to be angry rather than to be hurt.

She was angry at everyone. Herself. Her father. Her mother. Her coworkers. The stranger in the grocery store. You could hear it in her voice and see it on her face.

Learning to use the MAKE steps of comforting her own anger and other unpleasant emotions was the turning point to her transformation. She was so used to judging her anger as horrible and staying stuck. Once she learned to accept the anger, she then observed a notable shift and internal transformation.

She would come in and say, "What are you doing to me? I don't feel angry anymore. I feel so different!" She was doing the work. She was using the tools and becoming who she was meant to be.

She was better able to listen to others without lashing out in anger. She became much less critical of herself and others. She also began taking better care of herself. It was obvious she had elevated her self-worth and began to find joy in loving herself!

When we allow our emotions with self-compassion and acceptance, we are better able to manage our thoughts. When we calm our nervous system, we operate from a more intelligent part of our brain. Until then, we continue to be triggered and tend to react, and act out, rather than respond more maturely and intelligently.

"Anger is not a negative or positive emotion.
It is a necessary emotion, for those attempting to heal."
—Nate Postlethwait

MaxxExperience - The Feeling Letter

I found a version of this letter years ago and have used it for many of my clients. It allows you to get clarity on all the different emotions you may be experiencing. It's not necessary to give the letter to the person you're writing it to. The purpose is to give your emotions a way of expression, get clarity, and help those emotions transform.

Sometimes I even assign my clients to write it to themselves, especially if they're feeling a lot of confusion and lack of clarity within, or, various emotions going on at once.

Dear _____,

Anger:
I don't like _____

I am angry _____

I resent _____

I want _____

Sadness:

I am sad _____

I am hurt _____

I am missing _____

I hope _____

Fear:

I am scared _____

I fear _____

I get anxious _____

I need _____

Apologies, Love and Trust:

I realize _____

I regret _____

I apologize _____

I trust _____

I love _____

> *"There is one way of breathing that is shameful*
> *and constricted. Then, there's another way:*
> *a breath of love that takes you all the way to infinity."*
> *—Rumi*

MaxxExperience -
A Soothing Mantra and Your Breath

By now you are learning to use your breath to comfort unpleasant emotions and to help yourself move through the emotion. Now add a soothing mantra along with your breath. Pick just *one* unpleasant emotion you want to focus on today. Quieting your mind will help increase your awareness of your inner experience: your emotions, the sensations of those emotions, your thoughts, your wants, your judgments.

Set a timer for ten minutes. Allow yourself to sit or lie down in a comfortable position. Close your eyes and focus on your breath. If you notice your mind wandering, just bring your focus back to your breath. As you breathe in, imagine your breath going to the unpleasant sensations/emotions. Breathe in comfort, breathe out judgment. Imagine breathing in a comforting breath, again allowing your breath to go to the sensation of the emotion you are experiencing.

Now, pick at least one mantra below and as you breathe, repeat the mantra. Notice any changes. Notice which mantra is most helpful for you.

For anxiety:
Breathe in calmness. Breathe out anxiety
Breathe in peace. Breathe out anxiety.

For anger:
Breathe in calmness. Breathe out anger.
Breathe in peace. Breathe out anger.

For sadness:
Breathe in compassion. Breathe out sadness.

Breathe in nurturing. Breathe out sadness.

For grief/loss:
Breathe in compassion. Breathe out pain.
Breathe in love. Breathe out grieving.

For fear:
Breathe in courage. Breathe out fear.
Breathe in confidence. Breathe out fear.

MaxxExperience -
Write about your experience:

- Did you feel discomfort, relaxation, pain?
- Were your thoughts racing?
- Did you become more in touch with any certain emotion?
- If so, did you divert your attention, or did you focus on it?
- Write about any judgments that came up for you.
- Were you able to calm your unpleasant emotion (or emotions) with your breath or with a mantra?

Life is Meant to Be Enjoyed!
Feel the Positive and Pleasant Emotions

> "May we never forget the magic of being alive."
> —Sonia Motwani

One of the main reasons for learning techniques to heal and comfort unpleasant emotions is so you can experience more positive and pleasant emotions.

Often, we focus so much on the negative and we tend to overlook positive emotions. When you become more intimate with your unpleasant emotions, you will also become more intimate with your pleasant emotions.

You can elicit more positive emotions simply by injecting habits and activities that you enjoy. I think it's equally important to find ways to plan fun, social activities with people who are important to you.

I'll go a step further and say it's even more important to create these habits and plan these fun activities when life is challenging. As I mentioned in the introduction, my family went through a few years of great loss, tragedy, health issues, etc. It seemed to not let up, and I kept stressing the importance that we get together as a family and do things that were fun.

My sister actually died on the day of my parents' 59th anniversary. The year after her death, we decided to go to Las Vegas as a family to celebrate their 60th anniversary. Even my sister's daughter showed up as a surprise to my parents. We did this on purpose, to have fun as a family. It wasn't to avoid grieving.

Believe me, we grieved. We cried. We laughed. We connected. We did it all, and it felt complete, meaningful, and the right thing to do.

We needed to inject fun somewhere and somehow. Otherwise, life gets to be overwhelming and burdensome. Prolonged loss and stress can have a very negative effect on mental and physical health.

My brother has a funny saying when someone begins dwelling too much in the negative. He says, "Depress me later." In other words, enough with the negative! Move on, revisit later.

Creating habits and plans that elicit positive emotions is as important as being able to manage unpleasant emotions. There's a time and place for honoring grief and other unpleasant emotions, and it's not all the time. That is not healthy. It's important to learn the skills necessary to feel your emotions, accept them, comfort them, and express them. This is how we allow the natural flow of our emotions. They will come and go, and you will no longer need to dwell in them, self-medicate, suppress, or ignore them.

MaxxExperience - Create Habits and Activities that Elicit Pleasant Emotions

Think of activities, people, and places that elicit love, joy, calmness, and peace from you. They can be things such as cuddling with your pet, talking to a loved one, planting flowers, walking in nature, doing crafts/artwork, going to a movie, conversations with a stranger, taking a road trip, planning fun activities, etc.

Create your list below:

1.
2.
3.
4.
5.
6.
7.
8.
9.
10.

MaxxExperience - The **MAKE** 4-step process can also be used with pleasant emotions. Sometimes we don't feel worthy of positive emotions and need a reminder that it's okay to feel joy, love, excitement, and other pleasant emotions. Sometimes feeling positive emotions can feel foreign, and we may shy away from them.

MAKE a powerful decision to allow yourself to open up to feeling more pleasant emotions. This will help you break down walls and barriers that prevent you from feeling the fullness of your more positive and pleasant emotions.

1. **Mindfulness:** What emotion are you feeling? Where does it show up in your body? How would you describe the sensation?
2. **Acceptance:** Labeling the emotion is important. It gives a sense of acceptance.
   "I'm feeling my _____ and that's my experience."

"I'm feeling my _____ and it feels wonderful."

"I'm feeling my _____ and it's kind of scary."

"I'm feeling my _____ and _____."

3. **Kindness:** Allow yourself to breathe into the sensations of that emotion in your body. Breathe into the sensation and notice anything that arises as you allow yourself to embody this positive emotion. Write about your experience. Did this emotion make you smile, feel warm inside, or open your heart? Or, did it scare you? Were you uncomfortable with this feeling? Are you getting used to experiencing this positive emotion?

4. **Expression:** Use drawing, journaling, letter writing, or visualization to express your emotion. Write or draw about how you're feeling. If you notice yourself blocking off certain positive emotions, draw a picture of that block. Use music to help you feel your emotion. Continue exploring this until you notice a shift.

When we bury, avoid, or self-medicate our emotions, they will eventually come out as anxiety, depression, anger, or something else. If they're not addressed, they can become more severe and lead to mental illness. We are all human, and it's important to care for our emotional selves so we can also experience greater joy, love, and excitement!

Your emotions are your responsibility.
Judging your emotions does not silence them!
Dwelling in your emotions can make them worse.
Allow yourself to also experience and open
your heart to pleasant emotions.

RECAP: Managing Your Emotions

- Begin increasing your mindfulness (awareness without judgment) of emotions.
- Emotions show up in our bodies as sensations.
- Learn to listen to your emotions; they carry messages.
- Use your breath and focus meditations to move through emotions.
- Don't forget to experience and savor pleasant emotions.
- Use MAKE—the 4-step process to help guide you through unpleasant emotions and to help you discover any barriers to pleasant emotions.
- Extended periods of unpleasant emotions can be unhealthy and harmful to our bodies. It's important to inject positive experiences, fun, and love into our lives, especially when struggling through difficult times.

CHAPTER 3

Thoughts

You Are More Powerful Than You Think

> "The world we have created is a product of
> our thinking; it cannot be changed
> without changing our thinking."
> —Albert Einstein

In this chapter you will learn:

- The origin of your thoughts and core beliefs
- The consequences of not mastering your thinking
- The connection between your self-worth, self-esteem, mood, and behavior and your thoughts or core beliefs
- How to dispute the unhelpful, negative core beliefs, and discover your true self-worth and self-esteem
- The 12 common unhelpful thought patterns
- The ABC method of changing irrational, self-defeating beliefs that affect your moods, behaviors, and relationships

The Origins of Our Thoughts and Core Beliefs

Lexico.com says the definition of a thought is "An idea or opinion produced by thinking or occurring suddenly in the mind."

The definition of *belief* is "A state of mind in which a person thinks something to be the case, with or without there being empirical evidence to prove that something is the case with factual certainty."

Our self-esteem and self-worth stem from our thoughts and beliefs about ourselves. We create these thoughts and beliefs by our experiences and our reaction to those experiences.

Often, these thoughts about ourselves become our core beliefs about who we are. They become the dominant voice with which we operate in our world. We assume these core beliefs are true, and they go unnoticed and unchallenged for years.

Dorothy, a 70-year-old woman who had been in an unhealthy relationship with her husband for years, came to me believing several negative beliefs about herself. "I'm insignificant," "I'm not good enough," "I'm not smart," "I'm not lovable." You name it, she believed it. She had no idea of the possibility that these beliefs were perhaps not true. She carried these beliefs with her for 30 to 40 years.

We spent time working on increasing her mindfulness of "what is." Beginning with acceptance, she was able to then get curious about how she got to this place. With each session she gained more self-understanding. With experiential healing exercises she gained greater self-love as she uncovered more of her true authentic self.

By the time she ended her work with me, she exuded pure self-worth, self-confidence, and happiness that lit up her face each time she came to visit. She found her voice. She truly believed she was good enough, smart, lovable, and important! And, she shared it with her world: her community, her children, her grandchildren, and her friends.

> *Beliefs and thoughts are real,*
> *but they are not always true.*

They can be distorted, self-defeating, and debilitating. It is my belief that no matter how good or bad your childhood was, we all suffer from negative core beliefs at some points in our lives.

The good news is that when you identify and challenge your negative core beliefs, not only can you change your feelings, but you can also transform your self-esteem, self-worth, and how you approach your life.

> **We are all born valuable, worthy,**
> **and significant!**

Just think about that for a minute. We are all born valuable. We learn to devalue ourselves along the way.

You are valuable.
You are worthy.
You are significant.
You are honorable.

I realize you may not believe it. What I discovered in working with people is that I could tell them those things until I was blue in the face, but they didn't get it until they did the work: the experiential work of looking at their false, negative beliefs and unpleasant emotions until they healed their beliefs and emotions with acceptance and self-compassion.

Only then could they begin to transform their own self-worth, building the foundation with self-love.

We cannot change the past. However, you can change how you have been responding to your past.

One of the most significant and crucial factors is when you become mindful of your thoughts and begin fiercely questioning them. You can transcend self-defeating beliefs with wisdom and growth and discover your true, authentic self-worth.

Consequences of Not Mastering Your Thoughts

Have you experienced any of the following? Check off all that apply:

- ☐ Experiencing intense, extreme, or frequent anxiety, anger, sadness, guilt, or shame
- ☐ Low self-worth and/or self-esteem
- ☐ Getting stuck on the need to be right
- ☐ Lack of acceptance of self or others
- ☐ Rigid, irrational thinking that leads to need for control
- ☐ Lack of flexibility in relationships with self and others
- ☐ Underlying unhappiness and dissatisfaction with your life

When we are in emotional pain, sometimes it
means we still have something to learn.
Most times it's that we haven't learned to
love ourselves. At the core.

Our thoughts are extremely powerful. Thoughts fuel our feelings, our feelings fuel our behaviors, and our behaviors reinforce our thoughts. Here is a diagram of what that looks like and how it negatively affects our self-worth:

The Connection Between Your Thoughts and Self-Worth

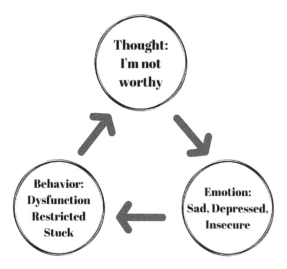

Benefits of Self-Worth

- Greater resilience
- Less reactive
- Clearer mind
- More decisive
- Trusting self
- More trusting of others
- Open heart
- Healthier boundaries
- Less anxiety
- Less depression

- Healthier relationships
- Higher self-esteem
- More self-discipline
- Overall better mental health

We learn to devalue ourselves along the way when we are hurt or traumatized. Trauma can be anything that can be considered a deeply distressing or disturbing experience. As I have previously described, trauma can be experienced in childhood with caretakers, teachers, clergy, religion, peers, and other adults. Trauma can also be experienced as adults in our relationships, our workplaces, and other communities.

Trauma is also along a continuum from mild to moderate to severe. It's a very personal response to an experience. As I have said before, what's traumatic for one person may not be traumatic to another. We lose ourselves in our childhoods, as well as in our adulthood.

People can also live fairly normal lives but still fall victim to these unhelpful, false negative core beliefs. This is why I like the term "rebonding with ourselves." Anytime we adopt unhelpful beliefs about ourselves, we have lost our way. What I mean by that is we lose ourselves. The way back is to rebond with who we were before any particular experience.

The inner child paradigm is a perfect example of how we learn to devalue ourselves, however, we also do this as adults. We lose ourselves in our jobs, in our relationships, in our childhoods, in the everyday tragedies and losses we experience throughout our lives.

We do this in the following two ways:

1. **Abandoning ourselves.** This is when we begin to devalue ourselves and put others and/or relationships above ourselves. We lose our sense of self. We lose our sense of importance and worth. We lose the connection we have with ourselves.

2. **Creating negative core beliefs about ourselves.** These beliefs affect how we feel about ourselves, ultimately affecting our self-worth and self-esteem.

These behaviors can impact our lives for years unless we are fortunate enough to make changes. People come into my office at all ages with the same dilemma, and my hope is to provide these tools and information to help alleviate this suffering.

Sometime in my twenties, I remember standing at a counter in a department store to return an item. The salesclerk was older than I was and was neither courteous nor pleasant. I immediately began to feel self-conscious, like *I had done something wrong.* I found myself shrinking into my own shame of even existing. I didn't even want to take up space. I wanted to hide or crawl under a rock.

And then, I became mindful of everything that was going on. What? I shouldn't even exist? *Oh, heck no!* I thought. I have every right to exist and return this item if that's my choice.

That was another turning point in my life and was so significant that I knew I wanted to help others to never feel shame for existing.

You have every right to be here! Take up space and do it without an ounce of shame! By now hopefully you're becoming more accepting of your emotions and it's now time to look at your thinking and your core beliefs.

Core beliefs are the self-imposed beliefs that we all have about ourselves. They are beliefs we have created as a response to our experiences in our world, and they are usually negative, false and unhelpful.

The great news is that when you cultivate self-compassion and understand your past and how you got to these beliefs, you can now change unhelpful, false core beliefs. You then practice installing true core beliefs that you deserve. Freeing yourself from further suffering, it's time to continue building that foundation of authentic self-worth through loving yourself and investigating your thoughts and beliefs.

Here is a small sample of common Toxic/False Core Beliefs and Helpful/True Core Beliefs Related to Self-Worth:

Unhelpful Beliefs	Helpful Beliefs
I am worthless	I am worthy/I am valuable
I am not lovable	I am lovable
I do not deserve love	I do deserve love
I am a bad person	I am a good person
I am not good enough	I am good enough
I am shameful	I am honorable
I am insignificant/ unimportant	I am significant/ important
I am different/don't belong	I am fine the way I am
I am ugly	I am beautiful
I am stupid	I am smart
It's not ok to show or feel my emotions	It is ok to feel or show my emotions
I deserve only bad things	I deserve good things
I have to please everyone	I don't have to please everyone
I have to be perfect	It's ok to make mistakes

Make a Commitment to Change Your
Unhelpful Core Beliefs Related to Your Self-Worth

MaxxExperience - Become mindful of what *is*.

Identify three negative core beliefs you believe to be true. At what age did you begin believing that about yourself? Write about the experiences that occurred that fueled your false, negative core beliefs.

1.

2.

3.

MaxxExperience - Accentuate the Positive

What are three more helpful, more true positive core beliefs you prefer to believe about yourself and your self-worth? After each one, write all the reasons why it is true. (I'm a good person because I am kind, I'm a hard worker, I'm honest, I'm valuable because I was born, etc.)

If this is difficult, think about your inner child and write all the things you like, appreciate, and love about her. Keep in mind, if you've made mistakes in the past that led to negative core beliefs, what would you say to a friend or child if they've made mistakes? You can make a mistake and still be a good person. Your understanding of what leads to the mistakes will be key in your healing. Understanding with compassion.

1.

2.

3.

As an Adult, Your Self-Worth is
Your Responsibility, and YOU Can Heal and
Change Your Thinking!

Self-Esteem

Self-esteem is what we believe we are capable of being and doing. While building my new coaching business, I kept struggling, and I couldn't pinpoint what was going wrong for me. I knew I was worthy of building this business. I knew I had valuable information that would help others. I felt I deserved to build a successful business. I was stuck until I realized I *wasn't* sure I was capable! What an eye-opener for me.

This is why mindfulness is so important. I could not change how I was stuck until I became aware of what the heck was going on. I then began to uncover all the unhelpful beliefs that revealed my uncertainty that I could not handle this new business. These beliefs were ones that fueled my self-esteem:

- I believed I couldn't figure things out.
- I believed I couldn't be successful.
- I believed I couldn't hire the right people.
- I believed I wasn't smart enough to understand the marketing piece.

Immediately, once I discovered all these unhelpful, negative core beliefs that were holding me back and keeping me stuck, they began to change.

I now had a choice. I knew I didn't want to continue believing those. I realized I could figure things out. I could learn. I could ask questions. I could get referrals to find the right people.

This was such a freeing experience for me. It was a turning point when things finally began to happen in the way I had been hoping and envisioning.

The Connection Between Your
Thoughts and Self-Esteem

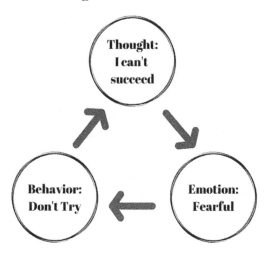

Benefits of having true self-esteem

- You face your fears, and you don't let fear stop you.
- You become more comfortable with making mistakes and being out of your comfort zone.
- You handle things better because you believe in yourself.
- You believe in others more.
- You learn to take feedback from others, without falling apart.
- You are more assertive in getting what you want.
- You set healthy boundaries.
- You are more resilient, and failing doesn't break you.
- You become more comfortable with failing and realize it is a valuable part of the process.
- You accomplish more of what you want in life.
- You have a sense of satisfaction, fulfillment, and purpose.
- You have fewer regrets because you try new things, and you don't stay stuck in your comfort zone.

Here is a list of common Toxic/False Core Beliefs and Helpful/Positive Core Beliefs Related to Self-Esteem:

Unhelpful Beliefs	Helpful Beliefs
I can't get what I want	I can get what I want
I'll never succeed	I can succeed
I can't handle it	I can handle it
I am a failure/will fail	I am not a failure/I can succeed/It's ok to make mistakes and/or fail
I am not in control	I can be in control
I am powerless/helpless	I am strong/resilient/capable
I am not capable of	I am capable of _____
I cannot _____	I can _____
I can't protect myself	I can protect myself
I have to be perfect	I don't have to be perfect
I can't trust my judgment	I can trust my judgment
I don't have a chance	I do have a chance

*Make a Commitment to Change Your
Unhelpful Core Beliefs Related to Your Self-Esteem*

"Our life is what our thoughts make it."
—Marcus Aurelius

MaxxExperience - Identify three unhelpful, negative core beliefs that affect your *self-esteem* and that you want to change. Write about the experiences that lead you to believe these about yourself. Describe at what age you adopted these beliefs and how these beliefs have affected your life. Write about how these beliefs have stopped you or keep you in your comfort zone:

1.

2.

3.

MaxxExperience - What are three more helpful positive core beliefs you would prefer to believe about yourself and your abilities? After each one, write all the reasons why it is true. (I'm smart because I can do _____, I can handle it because I've been through so much, etc.) If this is difficult, think about your inner child and write all the things you see she is capable of.

1.

2.

3.

As an Adult, Your Self-Esteem is Your Responsibility, and YOU Can Heal and Change Your Thinking!

RECAP: Heal/Change the Negative Core Beliefs Related to Self-Worth and Self-Esteem

- Mindfulness: Pick one unhelpful (false) toxic core belief that fuels your self-worth or self-esteem.
- Identify at what age you began believing the unhelpful negative beliefs.
- Begin installing new beliefs by practicing them. Write evidence to support each one. If this is challenging, remember how you might talk to a friend and do this for yourself.
- In addition, you may write letters from to/from your inner child at that age. Imagine what she/he would say about what she/he believes about herself/himself. Imagine what she is thinking, and what she needs. Write about what she believed about her own self-worth and self-esteem.
- Then answer each of these letters by writing letters of self-compassion to the younger you at that age. Tell your younger self what you think she's capable of and how she's worthy to you. Identify for her the true positive core beliefs about her true self-worth and self-esteem.
- Make two lists: 1) of all the traits and characteristics that make you worthy, loving, significant, and other traits related to your true self-worth, and 2) of all the traits and characteristics that make you capable, what you are good at, and other traits related to your self-esteem and your abilities. Write all the reasons these new beliefs are true.
- Practice, practice, practice the authentic positive core beliefs.

The Connection Between Your
Thoughts, Emotions and Behaviors

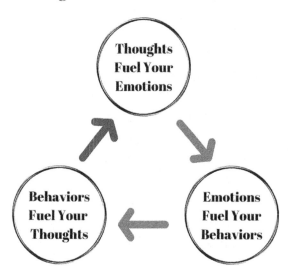

There are 12 common unhelpful belief patterns:

1. **Magnifying the negative**—focusing on the negative.
2. **Rejecting the positive**—minimizing or ignoring any positives.
3. **All or nothing thinking**—things are either bad or good, nothing in between.
4. **Overgeneralization**—using words such as "you never," "he always," "I'm always," etc.
5. **Mind-reading**—believing you know the intention of another.
6. **Catastrophic exaggeration**—seeing unfortunate events as catastrophic and dwelling there.
7. **Blaming**—blaming others for your emotions, thoughts, and unfortunate events.
8. **Assuming**—assuming the worst or assuming you know the outcome when you don't.

9. **Should**—demands we put on ourselves, others, and society.

10. **The fairytale fantasy**—life is unfair; things will magically happen.

11. **Mislabeling**—labeling self and others in derogatory terms (He's lazy, I'm a loser, etc.)

12. **Unfavorable comparisons**—comparing yourself to others in an unfavorable way.

Self-defeating thinking is unhelpful and leads to anxiety, depression, sadness, anger, and other unpleasant emotions, relationship difficulties, and negative behavior patterns.

The good news is you can change and modify your thinking. Remember, thoughts are not always facts, so it's important to become mindful of your thinking. Is this thought serving me? Is this thought causing me unpleasant emotions? Is this thought keeping me stuck or living small? Is this thought causing friction in my relationships? Can I change this thought? Yes, with practice, you can change any self-defeating and unhelpful thought!

Changing Self-Defeating/Unhelpful Thoughts—As easy as your **ABC'S** (adapted from Albert Ellis's ABC Model of Rational Emotive Cognitive Behavioral Therapy)

A—Activating Event: My partner continues to keep the lights on without consideration.

B—Belief: My partner **shouldn't** do this. He **should** be more considerate.

C—Consequence of this Belief (Emotions and Behaviors) Emotional Scale 0 to 10: I'm angry 8/10, I ignore him, and my anger leads to emotional eating and yelling at him because he didn't turn the lights off again.

D—Dispute the Belief: I **WANT** him to turn the lights off. I can't control what I think he should do. He is his own person, and he has different thoughts, ideas, and priorities. Category: **Shoulds**—placing demands on self, others, or society.

E—(New) Effective Belief: I **WANT** him to turn the lights off, but I can't force him to do something he doesn't think is important. I can't control him, and when I try, I am the one who is unhappy.

F—(New) Feeling: Less angry 4/10—I tend to let it go easier. I talk to him when I am not as angry and tell him I really **WANT** him to do this. The conversation goes much better.

MaxxExperience -
Think of an Activating Event from your own life.

Practice using the **ABC Method** to dispute the unhelpful thoughts related to this event:

A—

B—

C—

D—

E—

F—

Simple Hacks to Change Your Unhelpful Thinking Patterns

- Emotions are to be felt, embodied (see Chapter 2). If you're stuck in anxiety, anger, sadness, or any other unpleasant emotion, there is a good chance it's connected to an unhelpful, self-defeating thought.
- Anything you give energy to will increase; this is basic behaviorism. If you focus on the negative aspects of your life, you will increase your sadness, fear, anxiety, anger, jealousy, and other unpleasant emotions. If you focus on the positive aspects of your life, it is likely that you will experience greater happiness and more positive behaviors (more motivation, facing fears, less procrastination, etc.).
- Replace words like *never* and *always* with *sometimes* and *often.*
- Check your thoughts out with others when you can. We can't read people's minds, and we can't possibly know their thoughts and intentions.
- Take responsibility for your own thoughts, emotions, and reactions versus blaming others (e.g., "I feel _____ when you _____.")
- Replace *should* with *I want.*
- Stay in reality versus fantasy thinking.
- Refrain from using negative labels (stupid, failure, etc.). Work on facing your inner critic.
- When comparing yourself to another, be mindful that you are on *their* side of the road. Now, get back to your side of the road and focus on YOU and continue building your foundation of self-worth and self-love.
- When you build the foundation of self-worth, you'll naturally begin lifting others up, versus comparing negatively. There is room for everyone.

MaxxExperience - Make a List of Your Own Self-Defeating Thinking Hacks!

-
-
-
-
-

Your thoughts belong to you and are your responsibility.
Even when others do something that triggers you.
Even if something unfortunate happens.
Even when life throws you lemons or when someone hurts you.
Your thoughts are not always true.

RECAP: How Your Thoughts Affect Your Relationship with Yourself, Others, and Your Life

- Be mindful of your thoughts; identify your unhelpful thoughts and the categories they fall under.
- Understand the connection between thoughts, emotions, and behaviors.
- You are responsible for your thoughts.
- Thoughts are not always true or rational.
- Use the ABC Method to help dispute unhelpful thinking and replace it with more helpful thoughts.
- Changing your self-defeating thoughts can positively affect your emotions, your behaviors and your relationships.

CHAPTER 4

Healing

Loving Yourself Back to Life

> "We do not heal the past by dwelling there;
> we heal the past by living fully in the present."
> —Rachel Naomi Remen

In this chapter you will learn:

- The importance of a self-love practice
- There are many ways to heal
- Going back to the foundation
- The many benefits of compassion as a natural healer
- How to heal using letter writing to/from your inner child
- Consequences of Codependency
- How to use journaling for healing
- The Buddhist Meditation RAIN

A Self-Love Practice

You've probably heard of terms and phrases such as a "yoga practice," a "mindfulness practice," and a "meditation practice." Why in the world have we not established a self-love practice, or a psychological wellness practice? It's time to change that. If you want a stronger foundation of self-love, self-worth, and psychological well-being, you are going to have to practice it.

You have believed negative core beliefs about yourself for several years now; therefore, it will take some practice in order to change those beliefs to what is actually true. I tell people it's like learning a foreign language. It will feel awkward and untrue at first; however, the more you practice it the more fluent it will become. This holds true for every part of this process: increasing mindfulness, self-compassion, self-care, healthy boundaries, managing your emotions, and changing your negative core beliefs.

One of the ways to practice, as in yoga and meditation, is to actually set aside a specific time to engage in the activities. The other component of a "practice" is to focus on specific activities.

Consequences of *Not* Restoring Health and Healing

Are you experiencing any of the following? Check all that apply:

- ❏ Feeling intense and frequent triggers (an emotional reaction to something)
- ❏ Increased unpleasant emotions for a period of time (anxiety, anger, sadness)
- ❏ Inability to experience joy, happiness, or love
- ❏ Feeling alone and/or isolating yourself
- ❏ Lacking meaning and purpose

❑ Feeling emotionally exhausted
❑ Self-doubt and self-loathing

There Are Many Ways To Heal

Self-Healing	Self-Healing
Mindfulness	Letter Writing
Self-Acceptance	Journaling
Self-Understanding	Drawing/Art
Compassion	Writing
Meditation	Visualization
Breath Work	Nature
Emotional Intelligence	Yoga
Inner Child Work/	Exercise/Hiking/Biking
Bonding with Self	Healthy Boundaries
Reparenting	Self-Forgiveness

As you can see, there are many ways to heal and practice self-love—some of which you have already experienced in this workbook.

It's important for you to become aware of what works for you. Which experiences do you enjoy the most? Which experiences are most helpful to you? A very important part of my work with clients is to teach them to be the best experts in themselves. They know themselves much better than I, therefore, their feedback is extremely important in their healing and learning process.

The same applies with this workbook. I want you to become your own best expert in YOU. Therefore, pay close attention to which exercises and experiences are most helpful. Which do you prefer? Are there any that would be best if you had support from a friend or a professional? Part of building a foundation of self-love is knowing what you need and how to get it. What do you want your self-love practice to look like? How often do you want to practice these exercises?

Self-Healing	Self-Healing

The Foundation of Healing: Mindfulness, Acceptance, Understanding, and Emotional Intelligence

This is where it all starts, and you've already learned about each of these concepts in each of the previous chapters. I hope you see their lifelong benefits. They are the essential ingredients required to build and heal a foundation and sustain your emotional and mental health.

When life knocks you down (because we know it will) go to your foundation. Increase your awareness of what is. With acceptance. Compassion. Almost simultaneously, by using emotional intelligence skills to soothe, identify, and express emotions, you will then be able to manage your thinking processes more effectively.

The process to self-love, self-worth, and self-esteem is healing in itself. Once people increase their awareness of what is, and go through the experiential exercises of reparenting and rebonding with themselves, they not only heal but they feel invigorated. Often my clients will describe it as a weight being lifted off of them. They no longer have to carry the heavy weight of self-doubt, self-loathing, and shame.

The foundation of mindfulness and acceptance is where we begin to find clarity and wisdom. This is where we begin to find our higher selves. This is our way home.

Codependency: The Way to Emotional Bankruptcy

"Codependents don't have relationships, they have projects."
—Anonymous

In other words, codependents spend way too much time on other people's side of the road and not enough time on their side of the road.

There are many definitions and explanations of codependency. I like to keep things simple. First, as adults, codependency usually comes from being a caring, kind person who crosses the line into dysfunction and unhealthy behavior by placing someone else (or a relationship) as more important than themselves. Some people have more compassion for others than they do for themselves. This often leads to resentment or an empty emotional tank, and it can be a sign of codependent behavior.

Another description that is helpful and common is constantly thinking of someone else's negative behavior and obsessing about how to change it. These are the two most common forms of codependency that I have seen in working with my clients.

For a more in-depth look into codependency, I highly recommend the books *Facing Codependence* by Pia Mellody and *Codependent No More* by Melody Beattie.

Consequences of Codependent Behaviors

Are you experiencing any of the following? Check all that apply:

- ☐ People pleasing
- ☐ Needing validation from others
- ☐ Needing to be liked by others
- ☐ Difficulty being alone
- ☐ Denial of needs and emotions
- ☐ Insecurity
- ☐ High levels of guilt and shame
- ☐ Feelings of unworthiness
- ☐ Resentment
- ☐ Incessant worry over others
- ☐ Lacking a sense of self that is independent of others
- ☐ Difficulty making decisions
- ☐ Difficulty trusting self

Codependency can begin in childhood or in our adult relationships, where we, again, learn to abandon ourselves and be and do whatever we can to get the love and attention we so badly want.

Codependents usually have very poor boundaries. As codependents, we are more concerned and focused on others (or a relationship) at the expense of ourselves. When we focus on others, at the expense of ourselves, we operate from low self-worth and self-love.

Sarah came in with high anxiety and fear of leaving her house, and she was still living with her mom at age 29. She had become codependent on her mom. Her mom's needs became more important to Sarah than her own.

As often happens, once she began the work—with mindfulness, compassion, emotional intelligence and healing—of excavating the past and how it affected her, her anxiety and panic decreased. She began to build a foundation of true self-worth.

With this foundation she was better able to identify who she was and began doing the things that she was meant to do. She finally went back to school, something she had wanted to do for years. Not only did she move out of her mom's apartment, but she also moved out of the state!

The first step is awareness. Increase your awareness of how often you're focused on someone else and/or placing someone else or a relationship as more important than yourself. Next, get back to your side of the road. And stay there. Focus on what you need. What you want. What are your needs? How are you getting your needs met?

The next step is healing the past and how you got yourself there. If you've bought this workbook, it's likely that you exhibit some codependent behaviors and traits. You're in the right place. Keep working.

Compassion as a Healer

> "If you want others to be happy, practice compassion.
> If you want to be happy, practice compassion."
> —Dalai Lama

What is Compassion?

Compassion is showing special kindness to yourself and to others who are suffering. When we have compassion for others, the intention is to help alleviate suffering for that person. We are, in a sense, validating that person's experience by having compassion for them. They feel heard, seen, and accepted where they're at. As discussed previously in Chapter 1, this is the foundation of transformation. When we feel heard, seen, and accepted with who we are and where we're at, this is fertile ground for transformation.

*Compassion is a powerful healer
for self and for others.*

One of the things that is common when people begin working with me is they have no idea how to have compassion for themselves. Even with guidance, they get stuck and are unable to exhibit or imagine any compassion toward themselves.

We are often taught to have compassion for others, but how many ever talk about having compassion toward yourself? We certainly don't see compassion toward ourselves being modeled by those around us, so how are we to know?

It takes practice. Just know that, at first, you may not even believe a compassionate mantra toward yourself, such as, "I love you even though you're struggling." Give it enough time, and I guarantee you will begin to believe it, and it will become a truth at the core of your being when you develop a practice, as I discussed above.

Just like learning and practicing a foreign language,
when you practice self-compassion,
you will become fluent in self-love.

When you are able to have compassion for yourself, you will have more compassion for others. Most people, however, have more compassion for others than they do for themselves. This often leads to resentment or an empty emotional tank, and it can be a sign of codependent behavior.

Benefits of Self-Compassion

- Helps relieve suffering, sadness, fear, anger, and grief in yourself and in others.
- Decreases stress.
- Helps increase overall happiness, which boosts your immune system as well as overall physical and mental health.
- Increases your understanding of self and others.
- Opens your heart.
- Prevents isolation and allows for connection with self and others.
- Allows for our humanity.

Drawing

Drawing is another great way to begin the healing process. I often have people draw pictures of their hearts at various ages. They usually look at me like I'm an alien, however, I'm always amazed by what they come up with. I remember one man drew a picture of a heart encapsulated in an old ice box which was tightly wrapped with a heavy metal lock and chain. It was quite an amazing drawing and it helped him better understand himself. This is where his healing process began.

MaxxExperience - Drawing Your Barriers to Self-Compassion

What gets in your way of compassion for yourself? Draw a picture of your barriers to self-kindness and self-compassion. Use pictures, stick figures, words, phrases, colors—anything. Draw freely and allow yourself to express your thoughts and feelings without judgment or editing. Remember, the first step to change is becoming mindful of what is.

What are the messages about self-compassion you learned as a child? Check all that apply:

- ❑ You're not important.
- ❑ Your feelings aren't important.
- ❑ I don't know how to have self-compassion.
- ❑ It's not about you.
- ❑ You're being selfish.
- ❑ Other people's feelings and needs are more important than yours.
- ❑ It's not safe to open up your heart.
- ❑ I was never taught how to have self-compassion.

MaxxExperience - What Other Messages Did You Learn About Self-Compassion?

1.
2.
3.
4.
5.

MaxxExperience - Change the Old Messages about Self-Compassion

You now get to choose what you want to believe about self-compassion. Remember, the old ways of self-criticism, judgment, and negative self-talk DO NOT WORK!

You can now practice self-compassion through reparenting your (wounded) inner child and rebonding with yourself.

Identify 5 affirmations about self-compassion you can use when self-healing. Imagine what you would say to a friend or child and say that to yourself. You deserve compassion; you deserve love. Even if you don't believe it just yet. With practice you will! (e.g., "You deserve self-compassion," "I am here for you," "You are important," "Your feelings are important," etc.).

1.
2.
3.
4.
5.

MaxxExperience - Drawing and Letter Writing

Think of yourself as a child and draw a picture of your heart at age five. Age ten. Age fifteen. Age eighteen. Remember, allow yourself to draw freely and without any editing or judgment. You may use colors, words, phrases, etc. There is no right or wrong way to do this activity. Again, allow yourself to draw freely without judgment or editing. Feel free to use any age you are needing to address.

Age 5

Age 10

Age 15

Age 18

Inner Child Healing Using Letters

Getting to know the parts of ourselves that are hurting or unhealed in some way is powerful work. When you can wake up out of autopilot and do the personal development work, it's like having a party with a bunch of awesome imperfect quirky and brilliant people...your inner child, adapted adolescent, your shadow sides, inner critic and inner parent. Finally, you begin to celebrate who you really are.

Deidra came to me after years of destructive behavior and self-loathing. Frustrated with years of therapy and making little progress, she mustered up more courage and invested in herself and in my intensive coaching program.

Her transformation began with writing letters to and from her inner child, her "rebellious" teenager self and her inner parent. By getting to know her wise, loving inner child and her rebellious teen, she was better able to understand more about herself as a whole and complete person.

She discovered that her rebellious teen used anger as a way to protect herself; and as a result of this understanding, self-compassion began to replace self-judgment. By reconnecting with her innocent, wise and loving inner child, self-love began to replace self-loathing. Empathy replaced aggression.

Her heart was healing and she began building a foundation of self-love, and it showed in her smile. What a joy to witness!

MaxxExperience - Letters From Your (Wounded) Inner Child

Now allow your inner child (at 5 years old, 10, 15 and 18) to write about what it was like to be her/him at each of those ages. Allow your inner child to write freely without judgment or editing, speaking about her pain, her experiences, and how she feels about herself, as well as how she feels about others in her life.

Feel free to replace the age. For example, some people have experienced losing themselves in their adult relationships;

therefore, feel free to write from yourself at any age during your adulthood also.

Dear Inner Parent _____,

From my 5-year old self

Dear Inner Parent _____,

From my 10-year old self

Dear Dear Inner Parent _____,

From my 15-year old self

Dear Inner Parent _____,

From my 18-year old self

"Somedays, self-love will be an unspoken revolution just so quiet
as the sun brightening up the entire damn sky."
—Sonia Motwani

MaxxExperience -
Letters to Your Inner Child, a Compassionate
Rebonding Experience

Using the drawings and the letters in the previous
MaxxExperiences, write a letter of compassion, acceptance,
and understanding to your younger self at each of those ages.
Keep in mind, if it's difficult to come up with ways to have
compassion and understanding, think of a child or a friend and
what you would say to them. The purpose of this exercise is to
help your inner child feel heard and seen. There is no right or
wrong way to do this exercise.

This is for you to practice compassion for your inner child
(or wounded younger adult). When you gain acceptance and
understanding for your inner child (wounded younger adult),
it's much easier to cultivate acceptance and understanding for
your adult self. This is how you rebond with yourself. Things
you can say to your inner child: I hear you. I see you. I love
you. I'm sorry you went through that. I am here for you now.
These are just examples.

Dear 5-year-old _____,

Dear 10-year-old _____,

Dear 15-year-old _____,

Dear 18-year-old _____,

Visualization

Visualizations are another effective natural way to investigate challenges, gain better understanding, process emotions and heal. It's one of my favorite ways of helping my clients rebond with their inner child and become who they are meant to be. Feel free to record it yourself; therefore, you can listen to it at any time.

MaxxExperience -
Visualization: Bonding With Your Inner Child

Close your eyes and become aware of your breath. Allow yourself to quiet your mind and become present in the moment. Breathe in deeply and release the breath through your nose. Do this for about 3-4 breaths and then come back to your normal breathing.

Imagine your younger self (your inner child.) What age is she/he? What is she/he wearing?

When you feel ready, imagine bringing your inner child into the room with you. Sitting across from you. What is it like being her/him? Imagine yourself asking her/him questions to get to know her/him. Tell her that you are here for her now. That you learned to abandon her when she was young, and you are here now. Forever. To help her heal.

Remember, if this is difficult, imagine saying it to your child or a child who is hurting. The more you practice this, the easier it gets and the more authentic it feels.

I am here for you now. I see you. I hear you. I want to understand you. I hear your pain and I am sorry. I have compassion for you. I love you.

Tell her what you believe about her worth, her value. Tell her what you love about her. Imagine looking at her in the eyes and telling her: I'm sorry you are sad (scared, angry, or lonely.)

Imagine providing comfort to her for her painful emotion. Tell her I love you no matter what. You are valuable and you are worthy. (Use whatever core belief fits for you—You can succeed; You are healthy; You are important; You are lovable.).

Allow yourself to breathe into your heart—allowing the breath and the message of healing to come into your being.

Why? This inner child is you. You are her/him.

Allow the healing messages to come into you. Allow yourself to rebond with who you truly are.

Notice any changes in your body. Any relief or calmness you may be feeling. Perhaps you have released the weight of pain you have been carrying. This is truly letting go.

Is there anything else that you need to say to her/him. When you feel finished, imagine somehow putting your inner child in your heart, breathing in love, breathing out negativity.

I recommend *practicing* this type of visualization with your inner child. Each time you practice, it will help you feel more and more connected to your authentic self. Your true self-worth. Welcome home.

MaxxExperience - Reflecting

Write about your experience of the inner child work you just did. Do you need support from a friend? If so, who can you reach out to? Were you able to let go and truly heal, even if just a layer? Are you noticing any changes in your body? A weight lifted. More space in your heart for self-compassion?

Self-Care as a Form of Self-Compassion

I describe self-care as the ability to be mindful enough and self-aware enough to know what you need, when you need it, and how to get it. It's a sign of maturity to acknowledge that your own needs are important. This is just a sample of ways you can integrate self-care into your life.

- Learn to listen to yourself.
- Place yourself first. Remember, the most important relationship is the one you have with yourself.
- Learn to trust what you need.
- Learn to ask for what you want/need.
- Learn to give yourself what you want/need.
- It is not selfish to take care of yourself. (This is a myth!)

MaxxExperience - Make a list of ways you can begin to take care of yourself.

1.
2.
3.
4.
5.
6.
7.
8.
9.
10.

> "Feelings come and go
> like clouds in a windy sky.
> Conscious breathing is my anchor."
> —Thich Nhat Hanh

Ten-Minute Visualization: Using Your Breath to Cultivate Self-Compassion, Comfort, and Healing

Cultivate self-compassion with just ten minutes of silent meditation each day. Listen to what's going on internally. Quieting your mind will help increase your awareness of your inner experience: your emotions, thoughts, and wants. Allow yourself to sit or lie down in a comfortable position. Close your eyes and focus on your breath. If you notice your mind is wandering, just bring your focus back to your breath.

Bring your awareness to an unpleasant emotion you've recently been experiencing. Become aware of the sensations of that emotion in your body. Bring into your awareness the emotion, the sensation, and begin breathing into that sensation. As you breathe in, imagine breathing in comfort and compassion. Breathe out judgment.

Think about a time you felt this same emotion as a child. Imagine being with the younger version of you and exhibiting some form of compassion to her/him. Imagine holding his hand. Or rubbing her back. Imagine looking at him right in the eyes and saying "I am here for you. I love you, I see you, and I hear you."

You may begin to feel intense emotion...perhaps you're feeling empathy for your inner child. Try breathing in compassion for both of you. Allow this empathy to be there. It's okay. You can say to yourself, "I'm feeling my empathy and it's okay."

Continue breathing in comfort and compassion and breathing out negativity and judgment. Do this for several breaths. If your mind wanders, bring it back to your breath. Breathe in comfort and compassion. Breathe out judgment or negativity. Continue this until you feel some relief or calmness.

"If you are far away from yourself, how could you ever be close to another?"
—Yung Pueblo

MaxxExperience - Reflecting

Write about what you noticed. Give yourself credit and appreciation for the work you are doing. It takes courage to face some of these challenging experiences and less-than-pleasant emotions.

It takes courage to break the cycle of self-defeating patterns of avoiding, self-medicating, or repressing our true emotions.

Did you notice your unpleasant emotion losing its intensity?

Did you notice any other emotions coming up, such as empathy?

Describe the empathy and what that was like for you.

Were you able to have compassion for yourself and for your inner child?

Did you find yourself wanting to escape the emotion rather than breathe into it?

Or, were you able to transition into calmness or more space?

Do you feel lighter, as if you were able to let go of something heavy?

Remember, there is no right or wrong way to do this. You can use this exercise anytime when you are experiencing unpleasant emotions such as sadness, fear, anxiety, anger, etc.

MaxxExperience - Practice Self-Compassion

Identify three self-compassionate techniques or affirmations you will practice this week.

1.

2.

3.

MaxxExperience - Drawing Exercise

Earlier, you drew a picture of your barriers to self-kindness and self-compassion, the things that got in your way of being kind to yourself. Now, you get to draw a picture of yourself with fewer barriers. What is different in this picture? Use pictures, stick figures, words, phrases, colors, anything. Draw freely and allow yourself to express your thoughts and feelings without judgment or editing. What are the benefits of having fewer barriers to self-compassion and self-kindness? Do you have any fears? Does it feel more freeing?

RECAP: Ways to Practice Self-Compassion

- Practice self-compassion by breathing in comfort/love.
- Practice new beliefs about self-compassion, such as, "I deserve love," "I deserve self-compassion."
- Imagine what you would say to a friend or a child and say that to yourself.
- Heal unresolved trauma/emotions by writing letters to your inner child (or wounded younger adult), expressing your compassion for her/him.
- Using visualization and practice opening your heart to self-compassion for yourself.
- Practice self-care.
- Practice. Practice. Practice.

Boundaries

The Boundary Between You and I
Really Does Exist

Like fences that separate properties, emotional boundaries define a space and a differentiation between yourself and another person. Your emotional boundaries are the property lines that separate your thoughts, feelings, and wants from those of other people.

As you've probably already noticed, I explain boundaries with my clients as, "Staying on your side of the road."

Notice how much time you spend on someone's else's side of the road. Worrying about someone. Wishing they would change. Telling them what they *need* to feel, think, and do. Thinking they are the answer to your own self-worth. Believing they will fill any void or emptiness you are experiencing. These are just a few examples of being on the wrong side of the road! For a more indepth look at boundaries check out *Boundaries Workbook: When to Say Yes When to Say No To Take Control of Your Life* by Henry Cloud and John Townsend.

Ways to set emotional boundaries and have empathy for others

- I'm here for you.
- I hear what you're saying.
- I feel for you.
- Let me know if I can help.
- I'm too flooded with anger to understand you right now. I need to calm down.
- Can we chat later when I'm calmer?
- I'm sorry you're struggling; how can I help?
- I hear you. I see you.
- My experience is different from yours. I will respect your experience, and I want you to respect mine.
- We are two different people, and we each have our own thoughts, emotions, experiences, and perceptions. I hope you can respect this.

You are not responsible for other people's thoughts and feelings. You are only responsible for your own emotions and thoughts.

- Be in tune with your emotions and how to manage them.
- You're not responsible for others' emotions, thoughts, and experiences. Notice when you're on their side of the road and not yours. Get back to your side.

- Having empathy and understanding is healthy. Taking responsibility for their emotions is not.
- You don't need to feel guilty for how you feel.
- It's okay to say no.
- It's okay to leave a conversation if it's not safe for you.
- It's okay to leave a conversation if it's not serving you.
- If I were valuing myself, what would I do?

MaxxExperience - Practice Healthy Emotional Boundaries

Identify three healthy boundaries you will practice this week:

1.

2.

3.

Exercise, Nature, Yoga and Mindfulness— The Natural Antidepressants

There are many ways we can take care of our bodies that naturally produce chemicals that help keep our brains healthy and our moods better.

I've exercised most of my life. Not that there aren't times when I get bored, take a break, or struggle to get to the gym. However, without a doubt, the times I feel best in my life are when I am in some sort of regular exercise routine.

One of my favorite forms of exercise (and mindfulness) is hiking. Research reveals many benefits of exercise, nature, yoga, and mindfulness on our moods—not only decreasing anxiety, stress, anger, and sadness, but increasing pleasant emotions.

Here are some helpful articles I found:

Promoting Nature-Based Programs for People With Mental Illness
https://www.ncbi.nlm.nih.gov/pubmed/26985618

How Your Mental Health Reaps the Benefits of Exercise
https://www.psychologytoday.com/us/blog/what-works-and-why/201803/how-your-mental-health-reaps-the-enefits-exercise

Effectiveness of mindfulness-based cognitive behavior therapy on life satisfaction, and life orientation of adolescents with depression and suicidal ideation
https://www.sciencedirect.com/science/article/abs/pii/S1876201818311304)

I once worked with a psychiatric nurse practitioner who would write on her prescription pad, *"Get regular exercise,"* rather than the antidepressant du jour. I often recommended her to my clients for her more effective holistic approach. I believe these types of natural antidepressant remedies should be prescribed much more often.

Here is a list of examples of natural ways to help boost your mental and psychological wellness (feel free to add your own):

- Exercise
- Mindfulness
- Meditation
- Nature/Forest Bathing
- Diet/Nutrition
- Dancing
- Social Connection
- Giving/Helping Others
- Good Sleep Patterns
- Yoga
- Hiking
- Practicing gratitude

MaxxExperience -
List 5 Activities That Keep Your Mind Healthy

Make a list of your favorite top five activities and habits that help you cultivate a "Healthy Brain and Mind" then make a commitment to yourself by completing this statement: "When I value and love myself I keep my mind healthy by _____."

1. When I value and love myself, I keep my mind healthy by _____.
2. When I value and love myself, I keep my mind healthy by _____.
3. When I value and love myself, I keep my mind healthy by _____.
4. When I value and love myself, I keep my mind healthy by _____.
5. When I value and love myself, I keep my mind healthy by _____.

Letting Go and Forgiveness

There are also some myths about healing. Often, you will hear advice or directives such as "just let go" or "you just need to forgive." This is not only bad advice, it also doesn't work. Often, I have clients who say, "I thought I let go of that" or "I forgave that person years ago," when in fact, they continue to exhibit and experience enormous pain.

Sandra came to me after years of thinking she had "forgiven" her uncle of sexual abuse. She came to me believing there was something wrong with her. She felt sad, and this negativity was beginning to affect her relationship and her motivation in life. She was stuck and wasn't happy in her current job and had no idea where all this unhappiness was coming from. After all, she thought she had "let go" of her past abuse years ago.

With mindfulness, acceptance, and a deeper understanding of her inner child's wounds, she built a strong bond with herself and was able to heal her past once and for all.

Most of the time, people want to forget about the pain and the experiences that resulted in emotional distress, so they attempt to "let it go" or "forgive," hoping this will dull the pain. Sometimes it does temporarily dull the pain by sweeping it under the carpet. *However, true healing is what helps people "let go."* People cannot just "let go." It takes emotional authenticity and inner work to heal the wounds and truly let go of the consequences of any traumatic or unpleasant experiences.

It is the same with forgiveness. When it comes to forgiveness, sometimes we put the cart before the horse. People need healing before they can forgive. When we heal, we often naturally forgive. Also, forgiveness of others is not necessary for healing, and I believe it is a very individual decision.

Forgiveness Toward Self

On the other hand it is necessary to forgive yourself when you want to experience true healing. If you're experiencing shame or guilt, and are unable to release it, you may need to spend some time acknowledging those feelings using the **MAKE 4-step process in Chapter 2** and allowing yourself to process and comfort these painful emotions.

It may also help to write letters of forgiveness to yourself in order to release yourself from carrying this burden. Notice I say "letters." All journeys are unique—keep writing until you feel the shift of forgiveness you are wanting.

Shame and guilt are healthy when these emotions give us a message that we are human and have made a mistake...even if it's a very big mistake. You can learn to forgive yourself, or even ask for forgiveness.

Toxic shame is:

- Carrying the shame and guilt (for a mistake you made) forever, without forgiving yourself.
- Believing you are inherently a bad person for making the mistake, or for something someone did to you.
- Blaming yourself for something someone else did. This is called "carried shame." You are carrying shame that someone else should have carried.

In the case of "carried shame," determine whose shame you are carrying. Write a letter or use a visualization to imagine yourself giving that shame back to who it belongs to. You no longer have to continue carrying it. Again, write these letters until you feel the shift (and release) you are wanting for yourself.

It's time to release the toxic shame and forgive yourself.

I sometimes wonder is SHAME is a silent killer. Not depression. Not mental illness. Not addiction or alcoholism. Not loneliness. Not failure. But shame. Because it fuels all of these. What's the cure for shame? Accepting that you are human, and learning to love yourself...over and over again. To the next level. And then to the next...

MaxxExperience - Letter to Self

The way to release toxic shame toward yourself for a past mistake is self-forgiveness. Write a forgiveness letter to yourself (your adult self or your inner child). Again, if you find it difficult to have self-compassion for your mistake, pretend you are talking with a friend or a child. Write with acceptance, understanding, and compassion. The more you write and read the letter to yourself, the more authentic it will feel.

Dear Me,

Journaling

Journaling is another technique that can be used for healing. It's something you can do on your own to help you gain clarity, investigate challenges, and find solutions.

Here's an example of a way to use the MaxxMETHOD and journal through issues or challenges you may be having.

MaxxExperience -
Journaling and the MaxxMETHOD

Mindfulness
In order for me to become who I'm meant to be, I want to:

When I think of making this change or growing in this way, I:

Emotions
My emotions around this are:

I can become more accepting of myself by:

I can be more compassionate to myself by:

Thoughts
Some of my unhelpful thoughts are:

In order to become a more complete version of myself and continue to grow, I want to:

I can encourage myself by thinking:

Healing
One thing I can do today to begin growing in this area is:

I can get help and support by:

Own Your Dreams
This is important to me because:

If I don't try:

Do It NOW!
I am:

I can:

I want:

I will:

Visualization

I used this meditation when I was going through my healing process. I found it helpful for situations where I felt stuck. Again, when you allow yourself to fully accept where you are and curiously investigate, you find your own understanding, wisdom, and creativity.

MaxxExperience - Visualization RAIN (adapted from the Buddhist meditation and a popular meditation with Tara Brach)

The following is a guided visualization to help you transform difficult and challenging emotions and experiences. Read completely through the directions below and then engage in the practice in a comfortable setting. Feel free to read and record the visualization. That way you can listen to it at any time.

Sit back, relax, and close your eyes. Become aware of your breathing by allowing yourself to slowly breathe in deeply through your nose and slowly exhale through your mouth. Continue breathing deeply and slowly, exhaling slowly for a few breaths. Become aware of the sensations in your body: tightness, tingly feelings, nervousness, dull aches. Notice thoughts when they arise and do so without judgment.

Once you have become comfortable with your breathing, you will engage in the **RAIN** Meditation technique, by using the acronym RAIN—Recognize, Accept, Investigate, Nurture.

Recognize. What is the sensation, what is the emotion, what are the thoughts, who or what are they tied to? What is the strongest emotion you are experiencing? Notice the sensations in your body that this emotion creates.

Accept. Invite this emotion in. Become intimate with this emotion. Allow it to be there. Invite it in as if to say, "Hello, my sadness, there you are." Imagine the emotion sitting in front of you. Invite it in with compassion and imagine what it may look like. It may be a color, a shape, a version of yourself. Breathe in acceptance to help comfort. Breathe out judgment to release criticism. Continue breathing to comfort the sensations in your body and exhale any judgment or negativity.

Investigate. Ask yourself questions about the emotion. Is this feeling new or old? Have I experienced this emotion before? What do I need from myself when I'm feeling this emotion? What does my emotion need from me? This is a helpful question in comforting unpleasant emotions.

What is it that I haven't yet learned? What are my thoughts underlying the emotion? Are these thoughts helpful? What do

I need from myself? Does my inner child need something from me? Am I letting fear stop me? What am I afraid of?

Nurture. Find a way to nurture yourself, your emotions, and your thoughts with your breath. Imagine your breath coming in and providing comfort. Imagine your breath holding your fear. Maybe it's a simple statement that would nurture you at this time. "It's going to be okay," or "I can comfort myself." Imagine the love you have received from another person. Love from your grandmother, your pet, your partner, your father, or anyone else in your life. Feel any of those nurturing gestures in your body. Where do you feel being nurtured, cared for, loved? Breathe into that sensation in your body. Allow yourself to receive this nurturing.

When you are comfortable, allow yourself to go back to your breath and bring yourself back into the room. Wiggle your fingers and toes. Listen to the sounds around you. Open your eyes whenever you feel comfortable enough to do so.

I want to leave you with a few bullet points regarding healing:

- You are not responsible for the hurt and trauma that you endured as a child; however, you are responsible for how you can heal now.
- Our romantic relationships can be healing, however, it's not healthy to depend completely on a partner to heal your own self-worth. It's much more effective to do the work, heal yourself and build that foundation of self-worth. You will continue to heal in your relationships.
- You are so much more than what you believe.
- You are capable, and you can do it.

- It's healthy to reach out for help and support from loved ones.
- It's okay to get help!

Your healing is your responsibility.
Your past childhood experiences that were hurtful
are not your responsibility; however, as an adult,
your healing is always your responsibility.

RECAP: Healing is a Practice of Self-Love

- Establish a self-love practice.
- Get to know the ways you heal most effectively.
- Building a foundation of mindfulness is essential to healing.
- Self-love and compassion are natural ways to heal.
- Inner Child work is a way to re-bond with your true self.
- Use Boundaries for Codependency Issues.
- Cultivate a healthy brain and mind.
- True healing is the way "letting go." Forgiveness of others is a private and individual decision.
- Self-forgiveness is essential to healing.
- Be mindful of where you're suffering and make a choice to heal.
- Be mindful of where you are not owning yourself fully. Use journaling as a way to encourage yourself to grow.
- Invest in yourself and your own healing.
- Healing is your responsibility.

CHAPTER 5

Own Your Dreams

Be the CEO of Your Life

> "Tell me what it is you plan to do with
> your one wild and precious life."
> —Mary Oliver

In this chapter you will learn:

- How healing and increasing your self-worth will likely lead to bigger dreams
- To raise the bar for yourself
- To think out of the box, out of your comfort zone, and become the CEO of your life
- A way to inject novelty into your routines and keep life interesting and lively
- How to use Visualization to challenge yourself out of your comfort zone
- The 5-step process to accomplishing dreams, goals, and even small desires

Renewal: The Rewards of Healing

> *"When trauma is transformed,*
> *one of the gifts of healing is a*
> *childlike awe and reverence for life."*
> —*Peter Levine*

It's been interesting to see another trend in my 20-plus years of working with my clients. People begin getting in touch with their dreams right after they feel a sense of healing. It's one of the most rewarding things I get to experience in the work I do.

My family, friends, and acquaintances often ask me, "How do you do it? Your job must be so difficult." I'm always surprised by the question, because the way I see it, I have one of the most rewarding jobs in the world.

I get to see people transcend misery and suffering into greater joy. I get to see them transform depression, anxiety, self-doubt, and self-loathing into self-worth, confidence, and inner peace.

And when they heal, they begin going after their dreams.

Instead of drinking her day away, Melinda went to Europe for the first time and later found a job she loves.

Once Sabrina healed unresolved past issues and codependency, she not only moved out of her mom's apartment, she moved out of state and got accepted into art school—something she had wanted to do for years.

Patricia healed the relationship with her daughter and is now a proud grandmother who travels the world.

These are just a few examples of many!

When I used the MaxxMETHOD (not even realizing yet that I was creating a simple framework to help others), I began to dream. Once I got through the haze of my own grief, I found hope and possibility, and I began to dream again. For about five years, I had been thinking of transitioning out of counseling and into coaching. It took tragedy and suffering to catapult me out of my comfort zone.

Healing was the catalyst. Embracing healing was a step to challenging myself and fully owning my potential.

Own your dreams and let me know what you do. I want to hear about it. I love all the stories of clients moving fully into their lives. You have only one life to live—live it intimately, completely, and adventurously!

> "You're not behind in life. There's no schedule or timetable that we all must follow.
> It's all made up. Wherever you are right now is exactly where you need to be.
> Seven billion people can't do everything in exactly the same scheduled order.
> We are all different with a variety of needs and goals.
> Some get married early, some get married late, while others don't get married at all.
> What is early? What is late?
> Compared with whom? Compared with what?
> Some want children; others don't.
> Some want a career; others enjoy taking care of a house and children.
> Your life is not on anyone else's schedule.
> Don't beat yourself up for where you are right now.

> *It's YOUR timeline, not anyone else's,*
> *and nothing is off schedule."*
> —Emily Maroutian, *The Book of Relief:*
> *Passages and Exercises to Relieve Negative Emotion*
> *and Create More Ease in The Body*

I love this quote. I'm giving you permission in this workbook to dream big and live *your* life. Don't do it according to anyone's timeline but your own. We all have our individual journey, and that is to be respected, not compared.

This is your life. How do you want to design it? We have only one life—don't wait until it's too late.

When we do have dreams or wants, they are often stifled by negative thinking or fear. My hope is that you are learning skills to help you identify all the ways you stifle yourself and get in the way of your own dreams.

At the beginning of each session, I ask my client, "What do you want or need for today's session?" Often the answer is, "I don't know." Then, around the third session, they begin to find their voice, their internal locus of control, and they become more in touch with their own wants, needs, desires, and dreams.

Once we go through a healing process, a significant shift happens. There is more clarity and a desire to no longer live small. Suddenly, you become more in touch with a buried life dream, a passion, or even a glimpse of a new possibility. It's so exciting to see people at this stage when they have done the difficult work of finding self-love and becoming who they are meant to be. They now become excited about exploring new possibilities!

No more lack of awareness of your basic wants and desires. No more squashing your voice for others. You now have the tools necessary to increase your awareness, investigate and solve the ways you are stopping yourself.

This section is about allowing yourself to dream and live a life of no regrets.

The five biggest regrets from people who were dying...

1. "I wish I had the courage to live a life true to myself, not the life others expected of me."
2. "I wish I hadn't worked so hard."
3. "I wish I had the courage to express my feelings."
4. "I wish I had stayed in touch with my friends."
5. "I wish I had let myself be happier."

The Best Advice I Ever Got: Raise the Bar

So often we go through the motions of a ho-hum life, a mediocre existence. Before you know it, we've lived half our lives and wondered what the hell we have to show for it.

A friend and mentor once said to me "You need to raise the bar," and it hit me like a ton of bricks. I was living small in many ways, and he nailed it. His words often ring true in my ear, especially when I know I need to challenge myself. But I'm going to warn you. It gets messy.

If you want to grow, you're going
to have to get out of your comfort zone.
And, when you get out of your comfort zone,
it gets uncomfortable!

You will be faced with fears, self-doubt, and negative, unhelpful beliefs about yourself. Which is exactly why this is a way for you to grow.

Raising the bar gives you an opportunity to stretch yourself and become more of who you are meant to be by facing yourself and challenging every one of those doubts and beliefs that are holding you back.

If you want to stay comfortable, stay where you are.

If you want to grow, raise the bar.

The Importance of Novelty

> "Novelty is the great parent of pleasure."
> —Robert Frost

The opposite of boredom is novelty. I think one of the reasons we get on autopilot is because we don't have enough novelty in our lives. We get complacent in our comfort zones. Unfortunately, we don't grow in our comfort zones.

I'm gonna share a secret with you: I had been thinking of going into coaching for several years. While working with thousands of clients in my counseling practice, I kept thinking, *Everyone should have this information. It shouldn't be just for people who are fortunate enough to have access to care and then choose to go to therapy. I should write manuals for people and get this information out to the mainstream.* When I look back, I see how long I was in my comfort zone. Too dang long! I was on autopilot in my career and in my passion to help others. Don't let that happen to you.

MaxxExperience - Get Out of Your Comfort Zone

- Do something different for one weekend each month with your family, with your friends, or alone.
- Visit a new restaurant, hike in a new place, play a new board game.
- Drive a different route to and from work.
- Eat a new food, cook a new recipe, invite new friends over.
- Have new conversations with friends, partners, and family. Use open-ended questions to promote conversation.
- Make new friends. Have one older than you, and one younger than you.
- Find a new hobby.
- Make a list of how you want to grow in your career and do one thing that promotes that growth.
- Take a new class.
- Go to Toastmasters and learn public speaking.
- Join a charity organization or event.
- Do regular challenges with yourself and/or with others. Challenge yourself to do 30 days of only shopping for things you need. Challenge yourself to do something physical or educational that you normally wouldn't do.

MaxxExperience - Self-Reflection

Make your own list of things that will inject novelty into your daily life. Each week pick one and do it. Use this space to write about your experience.

Write about your experience:

What did you do?

What was the scariest part?

Did you face fear?

Did you have fun?

Did you meet new people?

Do you feel more confident?

What did you learn about yourself?

Are you proud of yourself?

MaxxExperience - Visualization—Who You Are Meant to Be

Feel free to record this visualization or read through it.

Get comfortable in a seated or lying position. Allow yourself to focus on your breathing. Notice the breath coming in through your nose and going out through your mouth. Take a couple of deep breaths in...and out...breathe in...and release slowly.

Notice your body relaxing as you bring yourself into this present moment. Let go of any stress or tension that you've been carrying today.

I want you to think about the biggest dream or desire you would love to have in your life.

The dream you long for or secretly have in the back of your head.

The dream that has been buried deep in your soul...or in the back pages of your journal.

If you could have anything you want in your life...what would it be?

That dream that makes you wonder *Can I really have that? Can I really do that?*

That dream that brings excitement and fear, all at the same time. That dream that seems completely out of your comfort zone yet brings tears to your eyes when you imagine it coming true. Allow yourself some time to imagine what that dream is, and what it would look like.

Now, imagine you being in that dream. Imagine yourself being that person who is living that dream. That relationship. That dream career. That speaking gig. That person traveling to that place you've been longing for.

Who do you need to be in order to step into this dream? What does that look like? Give yourself some time to think about this.

What beliefs do you need to change in order to fulfill this dream? Imagine yourself letting go of all of it that doesn't serve you in bringing this dream into reality. Give yourself some time to think about letting go.

Now think about the decisions you need to make today in order to make this a reality! What decisions do you have to make tomorrow, this month, this year to make this happen for yourself? Give yourself some time to think about the decisions you'll have to make.

Imagine each step along the way…

Now imagine it happening. You're there. You're that person you dreamed of.

How does it feel? Who are you with? What did you let go of? What did you conquer?

How are you different once you have accomplished your dream… different from when the dream was only hiding in the background of your mind or in your journal?

What is life like now that you made it through the discomfort of getting out of your comfort zone? What is it like to level up yourself in such a great way? Allow yourself to sit and revel in your accomplishment.

Dreams, Wants, Desires, Goals

What do you want to do with this wild and precious life of yours?

When we first began this journey together, I asked you to describe and set your intentions for this workbook.

I now want you to "Raise the bar." Write a new list. Compare the two. Has anything changed? What has changed? Are you allowing yourself to be braver? Have you cleared out limiting beliefs that held you back? Do you see other areas where you want to continue growing and transcending fears and limiting beliefs?

*Evolve. If you allow yourself to grow, there is a version
of yourself whom you haven't even met yet.*

MaxxExperience -
Challenge Yourself to "Raise the Bar"

What do I want for myself? Again, don't edit or think about money or other logistical matters. Allow yourself permission to see possibilities. **I want you to think outside of the box.**

- What will you do in your relationships now that your heart has healed and is more open?
- What's the one crazy or secret idea you've always wanted to pursue?
- What would you do if you had unlimited money and time?
- What kind of people do you want in your circle?
- Who do you want to spend your time with?
- What do you most value and how can you share it with the world?
- What do you need to do to give your life more meaning?
- What places do you want to see in your lifetime?
- What would you like to learn?

Begin Your List Here:

Personally:

Relationships:

Health (physical, emotional, and psychological growth):

Professionally/Education:

Hobbies/Fun/Adventure:

MaxxExperience -

Five Steps to Reach One Goal/Dream.

(Pick one to start until completion; repeat for other dreams/goals.)

1. Mindfulness: Pick one thing from your list that will be "raising the bar" for yourself.
2. Write all of the obstacles and then describe what it will look like if you **don't** do it. What will it feel like if you never try?
3. Think of the reasons why it **can** happen and write them down.
4. Break it down into steps from start to finish. How will you accomplish this dream? Set dates for each step.
5. Visualize it happening. Imagine yourself taking the steps. Imagine the obstacles; imagine the emotions around those obstacles. Imagine addressing each obstacle. Imagine all the reasons you can make it happen. Now, imagine it actually happening in the present. For example, I am hiking Mount Humphreys. Imagine stopping for breaks, eating snacks, taking pictures, feeling tired, feeling miserable, putting one foot in front of the other. Imagine dealing with each obstacle. Now, imagine how you feel once you've accomplished it. Visualize this until you accomplish it.

Write out one of your dreams here, using the five-step process:

I hope you're finding this chapter helpful in challenging you to get out of your comfort zone and raise the bar for yourself. I would love to hear more about your experiences and what you learned about yourself.

Keep going...you're almost through the finish line...do it NOW!

It's okay to want!
Want as much as your heart desires!
Then watch yourself as you get out of your comfort zone,
face your fears, and make decisions that allow you
to become who you are meant to be.

RECAP: Own Your Dreams

- Allow yourself to dream, to have wants/desires, and go after them.
- Become mindful of when you're in your comfort zone and avoiding growth.
- Raise the bar above your comfort zone.
- Inject novelty into your life regularly. Make lists of new things, places, and people to incorporate into your life. Implement the list daily, weekly, monthly, and yearly.
- Visualize who you are meant to be.
- Use the 5-step process to obtain what you want.
- Keep going...you're almost through the finish line.

CHAPTER 6

Do It NOW!

The Longer You Wait, the Longer It Will Take

> "Stick your neck out.
> It's a lot more fun than sitting at home and
> watching other people do it."
> —Sir Richard Branson

In This Chapter You Will Learn:

- How your shadow sides will stop you and how to integrate them
- How to feel your fear and do it anyway
- Why failing is okay and how it gets you to the finish line
- Simple thinking hack "I will do it"
- How you can use The MaxxMETHOD exponentially and for the rest of your life
- The importance of gratitude and how to have more of it

The Final Piece of the Puzzle

After my personal struggles and once I decided to transition into coaching and build a new business, I was faced with actually doing it! You can have all the dreams in the world; however, they are only a fantasy if you don't take action and "Do it NOW!"

And this is exactly how I came up with the last concept of the METHOD. I was hiking and wondering what in the world is going to be the "D"? I was also in the middle of feeling stuck in so many ways on my new business journey. There were too many things to learn. Things I didn't want to learn. People I needed to hire to outsource things I did not want to do. Finding the right people. My own perfectionism and procrastination tendencies that kept me at an impasse...and on and on.

All of a sudden it occurred to me: *Now I have to do it! Otherwise, this idea of mine is only a fantasy.* That not only hit me like a ton of bricks, it also completed the MaxxMETHOD, and there was no turning back. I figured out the keys to my entire puzzle, and to the MaxxMETHOD.

If I want something in my life, nobody is going to give it to me. It's not going to just magically happen. That is a type of self-defeating thinking. I have to do the work myself. I have to continue to look inward at all the ways I sabotage myself. All the ways I allow my fear to stop me. As well as all the ways I want to keep finding greater levels of functioning, self-mastery, meaning, adventure, and challenge in my life.

This is where the rubber meets the road. I had to become the CEO of my own company and my own life, and I had to "DO it NOW!" Now I'm encouraging you to be the CEO of your life and create a life that is aligned with your authentic self. Keep going!

Consequences of Staying Stuck

Are you experiencing any of these? Check all that apply:

- ❑ Living in regret
- ❑ Feeling incomplete
- ❑ Lack of commitment
- ❑ Lack of self-discipline
- ❑ Lack of focus
- ❑ Being consumed by envy
- ❑ Not reaching your potential
- ❑ Having no sense of purpose or meaning
- ❑ Allowing fear and insecurity to keep you stuck

> "An idea not coupled with action
> will never get any bigger than
> the brain cell it occupied."
> —Arnold H. Glasow

How Our Shadow Sides Stop Us

One of the most powerful exercises I do with my clients is a technique adapted from my training in Gestalt Therapy at the beginning of my career. I use an empty chair and guide them through a dialogue between the two parts of themselves that are struggling. These parts of ourselves are sometimes called our "shadow" sides or our "dark" sides. They are the parts of ourselves that we don't like or are ashamed of in some way.

When we hide these parts of ourselves in shame, disgust, or dislike, they stay stuck. As a result, we are fragmented and uncomfortable in some way. This is usually when clients come to me feeling a struggle.

They want a different type of relationship, yet they continue to participate in their relationship in a dysfunctional way. They feel bored in their careers because they are living far below their potential and not asserting themselves in some way in the workplace. They want to love themselves, however, their self-loathing has become top dog and their negative self-talk has become quite loud and frequent.

Guiding my clients through a dialogue between those two parts can be extremely enlightening, transformative, and life-altering. If you want to go further into examining your shadow sides—and there are many—I would recommend the book, *The Dark Side of the Light Chasers*, by Debbie Ford. I read her book years ago as an undergraduate and still, to this day, I am able to wrestle, and even win, with some of my shadow sides.

Amanda came to me wanting a deeper and more meaningful relationship with her boyfriend. She was terrified of losing him, especially if she showed him her "true self." As a result, she was constantly fearful, guarded, and unable to fully be herself.

She was extremely motivated because her boyfriend meant a lot to her, and she wanted this relationship to be healthy. The empty chair is a place where you have a dialogue between the two parts of yourself that are somehow at war with each other. Amanda had a dialogue between the part of her that was afraid and the part that wanted a deeper connection with her boyfriend.

The exercise requires that you move from one chair to the next depending on what part you are speaking from. This exercise gives you a chance to dive deeper into these two parts and gain a better understanding of them.

Right? It's such a simple, yet profound, experiential exercise that reveals so much. It allows us to open our awareness to parts of ourselves we would normally suppress and avoid in some way. It also allows us to get some balance between the two parts by giving a voice to the part that has been inhibited in some way.

This is an exercise in integrating *all* the parts of ourselves in a more balanced way. Again, when we become mindful of what is, change occurs, and we become closer to being who we are meant to be.

In doing this exercise, Amanda realized how much energy she was giving to her fears and how little attention she was giving to her desire to be herself around her boyfriend. This allowed her to see how much she liked the part of herself that she was hiding from him. Among many *ah ha!* moments, she concluded that she did not want to be with someone who would leave her for being her authentic self.

Possible Shadow Sides (Circle any that feel true for you)

procrastinator	non-committed	insecure
perfectionist	fearful	entitled
controlling	shy/timid	lazy
resistant	judger	jealous
lazy	fantasy thinker	entitled

Add any that you struggle with:

MaxxExperience -
Integration and Balance: The Empty Chair Dialogue

You can perform the dialogue using two chairs. Or you can use the space below to write out a dialogue between two parts of yourself (e.g., the shadow side "procrastination" and the "motivated" side.) I have provided an example below. This is a real-life example that I struggled with in writing this workbook. I hope it helps you see how we become out of balance and get stuck; and then, how this dialogue can help our understanding of our shadow side so we can restore balance.

Continue this dialogue until you feel completely finished. Feel free to continue on a separate page and perform this dialogue with other shadow sides as well. For the purpose of this chapter, you can look at the shadow sides that are holding you back from accomplishing your goals, dreams, and wants.

Procrastinator: Let's work on this editing tomorrow.

Driven/Desire to Succeed: You keep putting it off. Why?

Procrastinator: What if it's not helpful to anyone?

Driven/Desire to Succeed: I won't know until I try.

Procrastinator: It's a lot of work and that's scary, because what if you fail? (here the "procrastinator" side of me is protecting me from failing.)

Driven/Desire to Succeed: I don't want to live in fear like that. If I fail at least I know that I tried, and I can learn more about why I failed. If I don't try, I'll never know and that doesn't feel right at all. I won't be satisfied if I don't complete it.

Of course, this is a simplified version and sometimes the dialogue can be much more complex; or, like myself, you might have to have a few conversations. However, you can see how I was able to work out "the struggle" between these opposing needs/ desires of mine. As a result, my desire to succeed and complete the project was better able to take over and accomplish it.

Now it's your turn. Think about ways in which you're in a struggle with yourself.

Write out a script between the two parts of yourself that are struggling.

Were you able to find a better balance between the two? What did you learn about yourself? Is the shadow side serving a purpose? If so, what is it? Were you able to give a bigger voice to the non-shadow side? Did you feel a shift in integrating each part more fully?

Fear—Slaying the Dragon

Fear is a natural emotion, and sometimes it protects us from something harmful, such as a harmful snake, a dangerous situation, or an untrusting person. This is a helpful fear, and it's important to listen to it. It's important to also listen to fear that holds us back from living and reaching our potential.

> "All of our dreams can come true—
> if we have the courage to pursue them."
> —Walt Disney

Unfortunately, all too often, we allow our fear to become irrational and stop us from personal growth, and we end up living far below our potential and existing in small, unfulfilling lives. Irrational fear is unhelpful.

We fear emotional intimacy with others because we're afraid we'll get hurt. As a result, we are lonely and lack meaningful relationships.

We fear putting ourselves out there in professional settings because we're afraid of what others will think. We're afraid we'll make a mistake or that others will laugh at us. We fear we will fail. As a result, we live small lives professionally and live way below our potential.

We fear looking inward because we believe we may not be able to handle the emotional upheaval that might occur. Ironically, as a result of emotional repression, we suffer needlessly for years with depression, anxiety, anger, and other unpleasant emotions and self-defeating thoughts.

As a result of the above irrational fears, we lose the courage to live the lives we long for. We stay stuck in unhappy relationships with ourselves and with others. We work in boring, unfulfilling jobs because we fear that we "can't" reach higher levels of education, training, and abilities. We stay stuck in our own misery because we fear getting to know ourselves.

You are much more capable than you give yourself credit for. Fear will also help us reach our potential if we listen to it and allow ourselves to learn from it.

Did anyone teach you to stretch yourself beyond your wildest imagination? Who told you that "you can do this?" Did you ever learn that you are unique, and your individual desires and capabilities are there to explore, expand, and share with the world?

I often ask my clients, "What will your life look like if you **don't** make that change?" The answer is, of course, that it will continue looking exactly the same as it does now. In many cases, things might even get worse. Very rarely will things improve on their own without intentional action. If you want to live a happy, fulfilling life, you must decide that inaction is no longer an option.

In writing this workbook, I have faced many fears. I never saw myself as a writer. When the idea came to my mind, I thought I would hire someone who *was* a writer. This was my brilliant fear and perfectionist at work! I'll hire someone else to write it. I'll give them my ideas and they'll create a work of art. *Because, after all, you are not a writer. They'll do a much better job than you.*

Well, it didn't quite work out that way. To tell my story and to get my ideas on paper in an authentic way, I had to do the work myself. I had to face my fears and toxic perfectionism that would have held me back…if I had let them.

I got to know my fears and often my fears were very wise. I had to parse out the helpful wisdom and the irrational, self-defeating fears. My fear guided me to make certain considerations and decisions regarding the content. My fear wanted to put something out there that would be helpful and valuable to the reader. I listened to the wise part of my fear rather than let it stop me.

I am giving you permission to get to know your fears intimately. To face them. To conquer them. You have things to accomplish.

MaxxExperience - Cultivate Courage to Accomplish Your Goal

Pick one thing you would like to do that scares you. Write about what is stopping you. If your fear could talk what would it say? Listen to its wisdom.

What is the one thing you would like to do, but are afraid?

What does your fear say? Take heed and listen to its wisdom. Write a list of the helpful advice and another list of the irrational, self-defeating beliefs.

Write what limiting beliefs are keeping you stuck (refer back to Chapter 3)

Describe what it will look like if you *don't* try.

Describe what it will look like if you try and you will succeed.

Now visualize your accomplishment happening. What does it feel like to accomplish it? What will be different in your life? How will you be different?

Write about your experience in detail as you visualize it. Visualize daily until you make it happen.

Necessary Ingredients to Success

"Commitment is the glue that bonds you to your goals."
—Anonymous

Commitment—The Most Essential Ingredient

To get what you want, you have to know what you want and *commit* to it. What are you willing to commit to? Pick something that you are sincerely committed to and that is also doable.

Perhaps it's something that you have been putting off or pro-crastinating on for whatever reason.

Write it down right here...right now.

I am willing to commit to _____.

Now with some self-discipline and focus, you can accomplish your dream. Keep going...you're almost there. Do it NOW!

Self-Discipline: Helpful vs. Unhelpful Thinking

Do you know those people who get things done? People who don't allow themselves to get caught up in fear of anything. They just seem to do it. I've been thinking of this lately and wondering how some people have such great self-discipline.

To me, it seems they don't dwell in their fears. Like I said, they "just do it." What goes on in the mind of someone who is that self-disciplined? What is their secret? How do they take action and become so committed that you know—and they know—they will get it done?

For me, it came back to our thinking. Sometimes logic is so useful! If you want to accomplish something, don't dwell in fear! Simply commit and focus your thoughts accordingly.

I've been thinking lately about my resistance to finishing this book. My fears kept creeping up. What if people don't find it helpful? What if there are mistakes in the book that are missed? What if it gets bad reviews? What if people find out I'm really not a writer? What if I never get it done? Maybe I'm just not meant to be a writer.

I thought of other things I've done in my life that were difficult. I originally went to college right out of high school. I quit after one year.

Years later, when I made a commitment to return, I received a bachelor's degree and then a master's degree. I was so committed to this goal and extremely self-disciplined. I even graduated early by taking classes in the summer. I never got caught up in fear. I just did it. I knew what I wanted and nothing was going to stop me.

This was a bit of an *ah ha!* moment for me and the next time I began whining about not feeling like writing in my book, I quickly changed my thought to *I will work on my book,* and I sat down and did it.

The Connection Between Your Thoughts and Self-Discipline

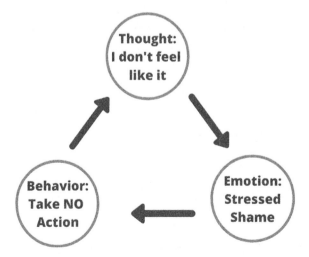

Unhelpful Thinking	Helpful Thinking
I don't want to... I'll do it later I don't feel like it I'll do it when I feel like it I'll never get this done I'm too tired	I will do it even if I don't want to I will do it now I will do if even if I don't feel like it I will do it at...(time) I will get this done I will do this even if I'm tired
Add Your Own Unhelpful Thoughts 1. 2. 3. 4. 5.	Change to Helpful Thought 1. 2. 3. 4. 5.

Think about your day-to-day experiences, and even normal everyday tasks and chores. How often are you thinking unhelpful thoughts that prevent you from getting things done? Now pick out one or two bigger goals/dreams/wants and write down the unhelpful thoughts that are keeping you from accomplishing and getting what you want.

Focus—The Ability to Hone In On What Needs to Be Done

There is more and more research coming out that concludes that multitasking is not only ineffective, but that it is harmful to our health. My suggestion: pick one thing and focus on it. What goal will you focus on? What task will you focus on?

MaxxExperience - Write a Focused List

Take the dream/goal/want/desire that you committed to earlier. Now, write a focused list of what needs to be done step-by-step, day-by-day. Put in dates. A beginning date. A middle date. An end date. Follow it as best as you can. Let me know how it goes. Focus. Focus. Focus.

Failing Is Part of Success and Part of the Journey

"It is not the critic who counts;
not the man who points out how the
strong man stumbles, or where the doer of
deeds could have done them better.
The credit belongs to the man who is actually
in the arena, whose face is marred by
dust and sweat and blood; who strives valiantly;
who errs, who comes short again and again,
because there is no effort without error and shortcoming;
but who does actually strive to do the deeds;
who knows great enthusiasms, the great devotions;
who spends himself in a worthy cause;
who, at the best, knows in the end the triumph of
high achievement, and who, at the worst,
if he fails, at least fails while daring greatly,
so that his place shall never be with those cold and
timid souls who neither know victory nor defeat."
—Theodore Roosevelt

MaxxExperience - Allow Yourself to Fail

I want you to begin thinking of failure differently. As a result, you will become less fearful of trying and more resilient if things don't work out. Make a list of what you consider past failures. Write the benefits of attempting or trying each thing that failed. What did you learn? What did you get out of it?

Sara Blakely, owner and founder of Spanx, describes how her father influenced her drive and determination in creating her business. She tells a story of applying for a job when she was in her twenties, and she didn't get it. She went back to her dad to tell him she didn't get the job, and he gave her a high-five and praised her for trying. Congratulate yourself for trying, for putting yourself in the arena! Big high-five to you!

The remedy is to face your fear and do it anyway. Learn to smile at fear. Learn to take it on, question it, learn from it, rather than to allow the fear to stop you. If you fail, you will learn valuable lessons, *and* you will grow. You will alleviate the regrets of living small. Begin thinking of failure as part of the journey. The more you get used to failing, the less fearful you become of failure. And, the more likely you will conquer your goals and become the person you were meant to be.

A Formula to Success:

Commitment + Self-Discipline + Focus + Failing = Success

Experience Gratitude: The Sweetness of Life

> "Cultivate the habit of being grateful for
> every good thing that comes to you,
> and to give thanks continuously.
> And because all things have contributed
> to your advancement, you should include
> all things in your gratitude."
> —Ralph Waldo Emerson

What is Gratitude?

The dictionary meaning of gratitude is "the quality of being thankful; readiness to show appreciation for and to return kindness."

Many people fail to understand how gratitude can change a life and alter one's perception for the good. The thing with gratitude is that it actually helps you much more than the person you're showing gratitude towards.

Sometimes, it's just a matter of feeling grateful within yourself and for what you do have. It's so easy to focus on scarcity, or what we don't have. During some difficult months in building my new coaching business, I often found myself focused on fear and scarcity. It was a challenging time to wake up in the middle of each night full of fear, wondering if I could succeed, and find the people I wanted to help.

One day I thought, *That's it, I do not want to continue thinking about scarcity: the lack of good people to help me with marketing, lack of succeeding to find the right clients to help, and lack of money!*

So, I began thinking and saying out loud all the things I was grateful for.

I turned this moment into an exercise of authentic gratitude. When I looked around, there was so much to be truly grateful for. It was another eye-opening moment for me.

It's so easy for our minds to get involved in negative thinking, and it's also stressful, depressing and unmotivating.

A life without gratitude is often an unhappy, unfilled life. Putting a little gratitude in your daily life is an important step in achieving many of your hopes, your dreams, and your goals.

> "Gratitude is the fairest blossom
> which springs from the soul."
> —Henry Ward Beecher

Philosophers and poets have long praised gratitude as one of the most desirable attitudes. Surely, each of us has much to be thankful for. Why not express our gratitude? It costs us nothing yet yields countless benefits.

Remember the section on self-defeating beliefs back in Chapter 3? In my opinion, one of the most important ones to dispute is "Magnifying the negative and rejecting the positive."

Let's face it, as I said in the beginning of the workbook, life can be difficult. Life is also beautiful and amazing. We can have relationships that are beautiful and amazing. If only we focus on what's good in the world. We all have a choice of how we want to see the world. I choose to try and look mostly at what's positive in the world. One way to help me do that is through gratitude.

How Can You Express Gratitude?

- Say a kind word. The quickest, simplest, and easiest way to demonstrate gratitude is to say thanks to another.
- Include others in your plans.
- Listen intently.
- Bring over lunch.
- Email to check in.
- Call to say hello.
- Ask if there's anything you can do.
- Pick flowers from your garden and deliver them to a friend.
- Be thankful for the things you have.
- Be thankful for the people in your life.

MaxxExperience - Make a Gratitude List

Think about *everything* in your life you are grateful for. Write down as many things as you can. Can you reach 100? I hope you have learned to have gratitude for yourself, the courage and commitment you have exhibited, and the positive changes you have made. And, I hope you're proud of yourself.

Lifelong Skills:
Use the MaxxMETHOD Exponentially

You did it! Congratulations! I hope you're proud of yourself for this great accomplishment.

Whenever you find yourself stuck, go back to Chapter 1 on Mindfulness and begin using the skills and exercises to address your current situation. The MaxxMETHOD framework is meant to be used as a personal development roadmap for whatever challenges and difficulties you may face.

I hope this workbook has helped you find joy in loving yourself and becoming more of who you are meant to be. Self-worth, self-love, and self-esteem are all concepts that do not have an end destination. You will continue to be challenged by life, other people, experiences, and unfortunate events. My hope is that you will have a stronger foundation, along with tools in your arsenal, that will help you continue to elevate your life.

Personal growth is not a destination. As cliché as it sounds, it *is* a journey. I hope you continue to use the MaxxMETHOD Workbook to help you along your journey. Feel free to check in with me and let me know in what ways the workbook has been helpful to you. I would love to hear from you!

RECAP: Do It NOW!

- Are you fantasizing about a goal, a change, or a desire…or are you committed to taking action?
- Explore your shadow sides and how they're stopping you, using the Empty Chair Dialogue Script template.
- Use fear to help guide you rather than stop you.
- Ingredients to Success: Commitment, Self-Discipline, and Focus
- Change the way you look at failure. Allow yourself to fail, it's a part of the process. What did you learn?
- Experience gratitude, the sweetness of life.
- The MaxxMETHOD is a framework that you can use exponentially. Keep using the exercises in each chapter to level up your self-worth, self-esteem, productivity, facing your fears, and accomplishing your dreams.

References and Recommendations

Beattie, Melody (1986) *Codependent No More: How to Stop Controlling Others and Start Caring for Yourself*, Hazelden

Black, Claudia (2018) *Unspoken Legacy: Addressing the Impact of Trauma and Addiction within the Family*, Central Recovery Press

Brach, Tara, *"Ancient Buddhist Way to Cope With Hardship: RAIN is a Buddhist mindfulness tool that offers support for working with intense and difficult emotions,"* Yoga Journal, APR 5, 2017 https://www.yogajournal.com/yoga-101/let-it-rain

Chopich, Erika J. and Paul, Margaret (1990) *Healing Your Aloneness: Finding Love and Wholeness Through Your Inner Child*, HarperOne

Cloud, Henry, and Townsend, John (2018) *Boundaries Workbook: When to Say Yes, How to Say No to Take Control of Your Life*, Zondervan

Ellis, Albert, "The ABC Model" https://en.wikipedia.org/wiki/Rational_emotive_behavior_therapy

Ford, Debbie (2010) *The Dark Side of the Light Chasers: Reclaiming Your Power, Creativity, Brilliance, and Dreams*, Riverhead Books

Gestalt Therapy
https://en.wikipedia.org/wiki/Gestalt_therapy

Mellody, Pia (2003) *Facing Codependence: What It Is, Where It Comes from, How It Sabotages Our Lives*, Harper & Row

Neff, Kristen (2011) *Self-Compassion: The Proven Power of Being Kind to Yourself*, HarperCollins

Sivers, Derek (2015) *Anything You Want*, Penguin https://www.amazon.com/Anything-You-Want-Lessons-Entrepreneur/dp/1511366079

Sivers, Derek, "No "yes." Either "HELL YEAH!" or "no." https://sivers.org/hellyeah

Zinn, Jon Kabat, https://en.wikipedia.org/wiki/Jon_Kabat-Zinn

Epilogue

> "Gratitude unlocks the fullness of life.
> It turns what we have into enough, and more.
> It turns denial into acceptance,
> chaos into order, confusion to clarity.
> It can turn a meal into a feast,
> a house into a home, a stranger into a friend."
> —Melody Beattie

One of the most rewarding things for me in all of my years of working as a psychotherapist and coach has been watching people transform into more complete, happier, and healthier versions of themselves.

Truth be told, they were already that way. That is their authentic self. I just helped them remove their barriers.

Thank you for allowing me to be a part of your journey. I am honored when you trust me enough to become a tiny part of your inner self.

I commend you for the courage to embark on such an intimate journey. I hope this introduction to the MaxxMETHOD helps you begin to see the wholeness of being in your emotions, your thoughts, and your dreams. I hope you begin to appreciate your amazing uniqueness and your unstoppable greatness.

If you have any questions about the MaxxMETHOD, or want to share your experiences from the workbook, please contact me at christy@christymaxey.com. I would love to hear from you!

Here's to self-love,

—Christy

Engage with Christy Maxey, MC

Workshops—Healing the Past, Building a Foundation of Self-Worth and Increasing Emotional Intelligence

Podcast Guest Speaker—Healing the Past, Building a Foundation of Self-Worth and Increasing Emotional Intelligence

Personal Development Coaching (Online and/or In-Office in Phoenix and Mesa, Arizona)

Group Coaching Mastermind based on the MaxxMETHOD Workbook/Journal

For more information go to www.maxxmethod.com